TOURING
TEXAS
WINERIES

Scenic Drives to 27 Lone Star Vineyards

D1372268

THOMAS M. CIESLA

Gulf Publishing Company
Houston, Texas

TOURING TEXAS WINERIES

Gulf Publishing Company
Book Division
P.O. Box 2608 □ Houston Texas 77252-2608

10 9 8 7 6 5 4 3 2 1

Library of Congress Cataloging-in-Publication Data

Ciesla, Thomas M.
    Touring Texas wineries : scenic drives to 27 lone star vineyards / Thomas M. Ciesla, Regina M. Ciesla.
       p.   cm.
    Includes bibliographical references and index.
    ISBN 0-88415-376-2 (alk. paper)
    1. Wineries—Texas—Guidebooks.   2. Wine and winemaking—Texas.   3. Texas—Guidebooks.   I. Ciesla, Regina M.   II. Title.
TP557.C5   1998
641.2′2′025764—dc21   98-14790
                                                                 CIP

Printed on Acid-Free Paper (∞).

Printed in the United States of America.

The Publisher wishes to thank the individual wineries, bed & breakfast inns, and restaurants for the use of their photographs. In addition, the Publisher appreciates the photo contributions from the Texas Department of Agriculture and Austin Convention and Visitors Bureau.

Publisher: Kris Jamsa, Ph.D.
Managing Editor/Project Editor:
    Joyce Alff
Performance Managers:
    Phil Carmical, Kim Kilmer
Manufacturing Coordinator:
    Shannon Yates
Production Director/Book Design &
    Layout: Roxann L. Combs
Production Assistant: Vanessa White

Cover Design: Laura Dion
Typesetting: Adelaida Mendoza,
    Cathy Scott
Prepress: Jean Alexander
Graphic Designers: Daniell McCleney,
    Senta Rivera
Proofreaders: Betty Loth,
    Deborah Shelton, Mary Gaw
Map Designer: Thomas Ciesla

CONTENTS

Chapter 1
About Texas Wines   1
The Formative Years—The 19th Century, 2. The Modern
Years—The 20th Century, 4. Recognition for Texas Wines, 6.
Looking Toward Tomorrow, 7. Touring Texas Wineries, 9.
Tours and Tastings, 11.

Chapter 2
North Central Wineries 13
The Munson Trail, 13. Homestead Vineyards and Winery, 16.
Hidden Springs Winery, 18. La Buena Vida Vineyards, 23. Delaney
Vineyards, 28. La Bodega Winery, 32. Bed and Breakfasts Along
the Munson Trail, 36. Restaurants Along the Munson Trail, 38.

ACKNOWLEDGMENTS

*N*aturally, when you write a book on wineries in a state the size of Texas, you run into a few folks along the way. The individuals that make up the Texas wine industry are by far some of the nicest people we have ever met, and we wish to thank all of them for directly and indirectly helping us with writing this book. Of course, we have to say the same to those folks we met along the way during our travels across the state. Whether it was a hotel in Dallas, a bed and breakfast in Fredericksburg, or a State Trooper in West Texas, the Lone Star State should be proud of the people who live within its borders—thank you all for making our journey safe and pleasant.

Of all those who helped along the way, a few stand out above the rest. A special thanks to Paul Bonarrigo of Messina Hof Wine Cellars for his encouragement in the early and final phases of this work. His gracious moral support along the way was invaluable. We also thank Russell Smith, Lisa Allen of the Texas Wine and Grape Growers Association, Tim Dodd of the Texas Wine Marketing Research Institute, and Susan Dunn and associates at the Texas Department of Agriculture.

To the vintners and grape growers of Texas, we say "Cheers!" Don't let that Texas pioneer spirit die.

If you drink alcoholic beverages, do so in
moderation and when consumption
does not put you or others at risk.

INTRODUCTION

*I*f you enjoy drinking wine, learning about wine, or visiting friendly places where wine is made, you might want to try something new from the Lone Star State—Texas wineries and the unique people and places that form the Texas Wine Trails. Whether you are looking for a fun trip with family or a romantic weekend in a cozy cottage in the Texas Hill Country, the *Touring Texas Wineries* has something for you.

What is a Texas wine tour? While the wine touring concept is an old one, the sheer size of Texas, and until recently, the relatively small number of wineries, made the idea of a wine tour difficult to imagine in this state where everything seems larger than life. The explosive growth of Texas wineries in the late 1980s and early 1990s has allowed us to outline for the very first time six wine tours. Along the way you will taste the wines, meet the people who create them, and enjoy the attractions of the surrounding communities. As you will see, it is impossible to separate the wine from the history, culture, and romance of the location where it is created.

These tours are a casual, fun way to visit Texas wineries and allow you to plan a day, a weekend, or a holiday trip through picturesque areas of the state. By focusing each tour on a small number of wineries, we hope your trips will be fun-filled and free of frantic schedules. You will have the extra time needed to personally meet the winery owners and winemakers to discuss their techniques and passion for winemaking. Then, after visiting the wineries, you can enjoy the shops and restaurants in the surrounding communities, and perhaps even stay the night to sample some good old Texas hospitality. The best of the Texas wine industry and all of what makes Texas itself so special can be experienced along these wine tours.

Who ventures along these wine trails? Reports from the winery owners tell us that just as many Texans as non-Texans are likely to visit these wineries. You will find singles, couples, families, newlyweds, retirees, wine lovers, and folks new to wine at these wineries. By the way, the smiles you'll see on the faces of these folks aren't from too much wine tasting, but from the kind, friendly treatment of the staff at all the Texas wineries. Texas winemakers are proud of their state and of the wine they create. This pride is probably best summed up in an old Texas saying: "Two kinds of people in this world, son—folks that live in Texas, and those not fortunate enough." A trip down one of the Texas wine trails will definitely help you understand that pride.

"Why take one of these trips? I don't know very much about wine!" One of the best things about a trip along a Texas wine trail is that you don't have to be a wine expert! You don't even have to know anything about wine. No one cares. No one will snicker when you ask a question or wonder what wine to serve with a meal. You no longer have to feel intimidated about tasting wine. If you are new to wine, folks at the wineries will be happy to explain wine and winemaking techniques. If you are an experienced wine drinker, traveling these trails will be a great way to find out more about Texas wines, and learn to appreciate the challenges these vintners face.

Perhaps you want to do more than just sample some great wine. Maybe you need a Saturday out of town, just to get away from it all. Or you may be looking for a romantic weekend with that special someone to enjoy fine wine, good food, and each other's company. Or perhaps, you are a visitor from another state, trying to decide on the best way to see this giant state they call Texas. The Texas wine trails can fulfill any of these needs. One thing is certain, you will come away with memorable wines, great food, and good times with the people you will meet along the way.

Where do we begin? Before we get too excited and start running down one of the wine trails, join us for a brief story of wine production in Texas. Remember that the Texas wine industry is a young, dynamic one. As it evolves, new wineries appear as quickly as others fade away. Though we have made every effort to make this an accurate collection of Texas wineries, it is almost impossible for any book written on the subject to remain current for an extended length of time. Keeping that in mind, we have created an Internet Web site, called oddly enough, the Texas Wine Trails. It will serve our readers to update listings of Texas wineries between revised editions of this book. The Internet address for our Web site is:

http://www.texaswinetrails.com/texas.htm

HOW TO READ A WINE LABEL

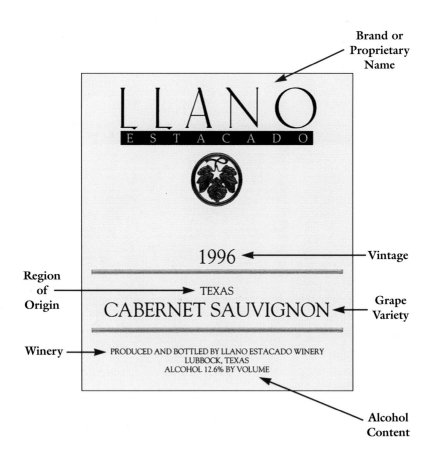

Brand or Proprietary Name

LLANO
ESTACADO

1996 ← Vintage

Region of Origin →

TEXAS
CABERNET SAUVIGNON ← Grape Variety

Winery →

PRODUCED AND BOTTLED BY LLANO ESTACADO WINERY
LUBBOCK, TEXAS
ALCOHOL 12.6% BY VOLUME

Alcohol Content

AWARD-WINNING TEXAS WINES

The Lone Star Wine competition, sponsored by the Texas Wine and Grape Growers Association and the Star-Telegram/Northeast, was held on August 28, 1997 at the Grapevine Convention Center.

GOLD MEDALS AND GRAND STAR AWARDS

Blue Mountain Vineyards: 1995 Cabernet Sauvignon
Fall Creek Vineyards: 1996 Chenin Bland

SILVER AND BEST OF CLASS AWARDS

Becker Vineyards: 1996 Muscat Canelli
Blue Mountain Vineyards: 1995 Cabernet/Merlot
Cap*Rock Winery: 1996 Cabernet Royale
Cap*Rock Winery: 1996 Topaz Royale
Fall Creek Vineyards: 1996 Chardonnay
Fall Creek Vineyards: 1996 Merlot
La Buena Vida Vineyards: 1996 Sauvignon Blanc
Messina Hof Wine Cellars: 1996 Late Harvest Johannisberg Riesling

BRONZE AWARDS (HIGHLIGHTS)

Cana Cellars: 1996 Muscat Canelli
Delaney Vineyards: 1994 Cabernet Sauvignon
Delaney Vineyards: 1995 Barrel-fermented Chardonnay
Fredericksburg Winery: 1996 Vertag
Grape Creek Vineyards: 1996 Cabernet Trois
Piney Woods Country Wines: NV Blueberry Wine
Piney Woods Country Wines: 1996 Muscadine Blush
Llano Estacado Winery: NV Port
Llano Estacado Winery: 1996 Blush

WINE TASTING

The difference between tasting wine and drinking wine revolves around how much attention you pay to the wine. Here's a few examples to show you the difference.

You're poolside on a hot Texas afternoon with a glass of iced-down Ste. Genevieve White Zinfandel by your side. It's 100° in the sun, you're thirsty, so you reach for the glass and take a big refreshing gulp. That's *drinking* wine!

You're at a party. The host pours you a glass of Pheasant Ridge Pinot Noir that you sip and say, "Mmmm, that's nice." Then for the remainder of the evening, you take a sip now and then while engaged in conversation. That's *drinking* wine!

You're at a tasting room of a Texas winery. A dozen or so people are huddled around the wine bar as the vintner holds two glasses of Chardonnay in the light so everyone can see the subtle differences in color. The vintner explains the one Chardonnay has undergone barrel fermentation and the other has not. Oak aging imparts a slightly darker hue to the wine. He pours a small sample of each for everyone and asks them to taste and comment on the difference between the two. That's *tasting* wine!

The obvious difference between the first two examples and the last one is the wine drinker's focus. When wine is a prop in a larger production (such as the pool or party), it is impossible to concentrate on the smells and tastes within the wine.

There are five basic steps to use when visiting a tasting room that will make it seem as though you've done this a thousand times. These steps that focus on the senses of sight, smell, and taste, include color, swirl, smell, taste, and savor.

Color—It's the first thing we notice about a wine, isn't it? If you are new to wine you may simply be able to tell if it's a white, blush, or red wine when you hold the glass. After some experience the color might tell you if it's a young or an aged wine. White wines gain color as they get older, and red wines lose color. Other wines like Zinfandels (not white Zinfandels) have a deep, almost purple color, and are sometimes called the "inky" Zins.

Swirl—Have you ever wondered why people swirl their wine? Are they just trying to look cool and sophisticated? Well, maybe some of them are, but swirling actually releases compounds from the wine allowing them to react with oxygen that enhances the "nose" of the wine. The "nose" is the combination of the aroma and bouquet each wine carries as a clue to the grapes and the winemaking process that produced the wine.

Swirling is easy to do, but use small motions, taking care not to "swirl" onto your tasting partner. There is of course a danger with swirling that we should mention. As you become adept at the motion you'll find yourself swirling everything! My wife has caught me on many occasions absent-mindedly swirling milk that I've poured into a wine glass.

Smell—Now that you have the swirling part down pat, we examine the reason for the swirl: the "nose." Most of us don't spend enough time at this stage, which is a pity, because as with most foods, wine usually tastes the way it smells. Take your time, we recommend bringing the glass of wine up to your nose at least twice before tasting. Remember the longer the wine is exposed to the air, the more changes occur in the "nose." Compounds in the wine create the wine's "signature," be it woody, fruity, vinegary, or like "burnt matches." As your experience grows, you may eventually be able to use these clues to identify bad wine *before* you taste it. And life is too short to drink bad wine!

Taste—Finally, we get to taste this stuff! Remember though, we're not *drinking* the wine, we're tasting. Take a small sip and hold it in your mouth for a moment. Different parts of the tongue are sensitive to different tastes. For example, the tip of the tongue contains the cells that recognize sweet tastes. For red wines or oak-aged white wines, you'll want the wine to swish around to the sides and center of the tongue to judge the amount of acidity or tannin flavors. Remember too, that wine is a complex substance and often contains more than one of these flavors in one sip. About 20 seconds after you've tasted the wine, a distinct aftertaste may linger, quite different from your initial taste. Really good wines will have a pleasing aftertaste.

Savor—You've looked, swirled, smelled, and finally tasted the wine. Now what? It may have seemed like a lot of work but in reality all four steps probably took only 30–40 seconds total. Now you have to ask yourself if you liked the wine. Is it a wine you would buy for yourself? What was it about the wine that you liked or didn't like? Was it too acidic? ("It tastes like a battery.") Was it too sweet? ("It tastes like a spoonful of sugar.") This reflection on what you just tasted will help you in future tastings and wine purchases. Finally, is the wine worth the price?

A NOTE ABOUT THE LOVE-HATE RELATIONSHIP BETWEEN OXYGEN AND WINE

During the winemaking process, oxygen is the devil for a vintner. Too large of a surface area exposed to oxygen inside of a barrel will ruin the wine. That is why vintners are constantly "topping off" barrels during the fermentation process to keep the amount of wine exposed to oxygen as small as possible.

For the consumer however, oxygen is the wines' friend—at least temporarily. Swirling a glass of wine to allow oxygen to mix with it is similar to removing the cork from a bottle in advance of pouring—allowing the wine to "breath." You can try this at home. Open a bottle of wine and immediately taste a small amount. Taste another sample after the bottle has remained open for 10–15 minutes. You'll be amazed at the difference.

But there is still a dark side to oxygen. The benefits gained from that initial contact with the air when you open a wine bottle will be overshadowed by the forces set in motion to spoil the wine. If you have wine remaining in a bottle and want to save it, refrigerate it as soon as possible to slow the spoiling process. You can expect wine to stay drinkable for up to a week when refrigerated. Left on a countertop, you won't like the flavor within just a few days.

Buying Texas Wines

Ten Do's and Don'ts for the Informed Wine Traveler

Chances are that as you travel these wine trails you will find yourself carrying home a few bottles of Texas wine—we always do even though we've traveled these trails many times. Here are a few tricks we've learned over the years.

DO purchase one of the cardboard wine carriers if available at the winery. They are a convenient way to carry and pack bottles of wine and reduce the chance of breakage.

DO leave sufficient room in the trunk for extra wine bottles, especially if you plan on buying a case or more.

DO ask the winery staff about distribution of their wines. Many of the smaller wineries only sell from the tasting room or in the local town. If you taste a wine from a small winery that you enjoy, but it! Chances are it will not be available in your hometown.

DO plan for the future. As you sample these wines think about the next six months. Will you be giving a dinner or a barbecue for friends? Is there a special occasion coming up such as a birthday or anniversary? A Texas wine would go nicely with any of these.

DO ship home the larger wine accessories you purchase in the tasting rooms. Some wineries offer a broad selection of wine accessories such as handmade wine racks, which can be quite large. Ship the accessories home to save trunk space for the wine.

DON'T take the smallest vehicle you own or rent a compact car. In addition to the items available in the wineries, each trail offers many shopping opportunities. For example, during one innocent trip along the Enchanted Trail, we came home with a butcher block table for the kitchen that we bought in Fredericksburg!

DON'T forget the strength of the Texas sun. Summertime temperatures in automobiles can ruin a wine in a matter of hours.

DON'T buy wine before you shop. If you are visiting wineries located in historic downtown districts such as Grapevine or Fredericksburg, it's likely that you will want to walk around to visit local shops and restaurants. Purchase your wine at the end of the day or have the winery hold your purchase until you return. One or two bottles of wine will feel ten times heavier after being carried around town for hours.

DON'T travel with open bottles in your automobile. If you've enjoyed a Texas wine while staying in your Bed and Breakfast or hotel room and would like to take the rest home, cork the bottle firmly and place it in your trunk. Do not carry an opened bottle of any alcoholic beverage with you in the passenger compartment.

DON'T be afraid to ask about personalized wine labels. Most Texas wineries now offer their customers the ability to purchase select wines with labels personalized for special occasions.

Chapter 1

ABOUT TEXAS WINES

*M*any of us today are startled when we hear that Texas has a wine industry. When most Americans think of Texas, they think of horses, cowboys, cattle, or oil, not wine and vineyards. The phenomenal growth of the Texas wine industry during the last few decades was preceded by a winemaking history dating back to the mid-1600s.

THE BEGINNINGS—17TH AND 18TH CENTURIES

By 1650 Spanish Franciscan monks had established a viticulture hold in the area around Paso Del Norte, which is now El Paso, by planting the Spanish black grape. This grape was hardy enough to grow in the Texas environment and produced a palatable wine. The monks did not think that wines made from native wild grapes were suitable for consumption. However, a readily available water supply and the development of irrigation systems made it possible for them to maintain extensive vineyards of the Spanish black grape.

In 1680 the Pueblo Revolt in the territory of New Mexico forced the Spaniards to flee for their lives and settle into the area now known as El Paso. The countryside, rich with flood plain

◀ THE CLEAR SIMPLE BEAUTY OF A GLASS OF TEXAS WINE.
(COURTESY OF THE TEXAS DEPARTMENT OF AGRICULTURE)

1

soil and adequate water, was turned into a garden paradise of fruit trees and vineyards that supplied the local missions with sacramental wines. These vineyards flourished throughout the eighteenth century and produced wines and brandy. In the early nineteenth century, however, objections were beginning to be raised concerning the quality of the wines from the El Paso area. As American wine consumers became increasingly familiar with the taste of vinifera-based wines, the flavor of wines based on native grapes became less desirable. At the same time, many growers were beginning to discover that few of the European vinifera grape varieties were capable of surviving the harsh environment of far West Texas.

THE FORMATIVE YEARS—THE 19TH CENTURY

Around the same time that West Texas was seeing a decrease in vineyard acreage, a second wave of European immigrants began to populate the Hill Country and northeast areas of Texas. German immigrants settled into the central Texas Hill Country and quickly established vineyards and wineries. The Steinberger Winery operated in this area of Texas from 1880 until the Prohibition.

As German immigrants were settling the Hill Country, Italian immigrants were settling into the eastern half of Texas. They too brought a heritage of winemaking with them by importing grapes from California to produce homemade wine. Northern Italians began to settle in the areas northwest of Dallas and established vineyards and orchards. The Carminati Winery operated from 1887 to 1919 and the Fenoglio Winery existed from 1900 to the Prohibition in 1919. The Fenoglios were influenced by T. V. Munson whose work with viticulture eventually saved the French wine industry. Using standard Concord grapes and Munson-developed hybrids, the Fenoglios produced first-class wines from an increasingly prolific grape producing area.

The Prohibition Act in the United States broke the back of the wine industry in Texas, closing all but one winery—Val Verde Winery in Del Rio, Texas. Val Verde was established by the Qualia fam-

TYPICAL TRELLIS WORK USED IN TEXAS VINEYARDS.
(COURTESY OF THE TEXAS DEPARTMENT OF AGRICULTURE)

ily in 1883. Unlike other wineries around the state, the Qualias continued to maintain their vineyard, using their grapes for jellies, jams, sacramental wines, and table grapes. Their grapes were hardy enough to withstand rail shipment to major centers such as Galveston and Houston. Although the Prohibition brought a close to an era for commercial winemaking in Texas, the time between the Civil War and the Prohibition served as a foundation for the winemakers that were to follow.

Three generations of the Qualia family and the work they performed with a variety of grapes after the Prohibition provided a critical link between past winemaking efforts and today's commercial wine industry in Texas.

Two experts in the field of raising grapes and making wines lived in Texas during this formative era. A. J. Winkler, born in Waco, went on to head the Department of Viticulture and Enology for thirty years at the University of California at Davis. The other internationally known authority was T. V. Munson. After a decade of researching, categorizing, and experimenting, Mr. Munson established a vineyard near Denison, where he classified over 300 varieties of grapes. His goal was to determine the best native grape rootstock onto which he could graft the European vinifera.

In the late 1800s, France's vineyards were devastated by the plant louse, *phylloxera*, which was introduced into France accidentally by Americans in the 1860s. Hearing of Munson's work, the French sent representatives to consult with the Texas expert. The French representative returned to France with disease-resistant Texas rootstock on which the French grafted their vines. French wines, which are so popular today, owe a large debt to native Texas rootstock.

Today you can visit the T. V. Munson Memorial Vineyard at Grayson County College in Denison, Texas. This vineyard was established in 1979 as a memorial and as a viticulture center. Grayson County College serves the Texas wine industry as a viticulture and enology center of education. Call for class information or visit them on their Web site: www.grayson.edu.

THE MODERN YEARS—THE 20TH CENTURY

By the early twentieth century, the vast vineyards of the El Paso area had disappeared. Nature and economics played a role in the demise of these vineyards. Floods devastated the crops, and raising vegetables to feed an increasing population became more profitable. El Paso's last winery, Isleta Winery, closed its doors in 1919, after more than eighty years of operation.

Research efforts around the state continued between the 1940s and the early 1960s and produced a renewed promise and interest in Texas grape production. California entered the wine industry in the 1960s and America discovered wine in the 1970s. So where was Texas? Texas winemakers were cautiously learning about growing grapes in Texas. It is true that Texas rootstock is resistant to *phylloxera*, but it has other enemies such as cottonroot rot and Pierce's disease that can destroy a vineyard in short order. Combine these diseases with the excitable weather in Texas and, if you are not cautious, you have a recipe for easy disaster.

However, Texans have always been famous for their pioneer spirit. That same tough determination they used to make oil flow

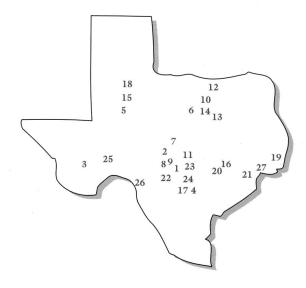

1. Becker Vineyards
2. Bell Mountain Vineyards
3. Blue Mountain Vineyards
4. Cana Cellars Winery
5. Cap*Rock Winery
6. Delaney Vineyards
7. Fall Creek Vineyards
8. Fredericksburg Winery
9. Grape Creek Vineyards
10. Hidden Springs Winery
11. Hill Country Cellars
12. Homestead Vineyards & Winery
13. Labodega Winery
14. LaBuena Vida Vineyards
15. Llano Estacado Winery
16. Messina Hof Wine Cellar
17. Oak Hill Cellars
18. Pheasant Ridge Winery
19. Piney Woods Country Winery
20. Pleasant Hill Winery
21. Red River Winery
22. Sister Creek Vineyards
23. Slaughter-Leftwich Vineyards
24. Spicewood Vineyards
25. Ste. Genevieve Winery
26. Val Verde Winery
27. Wimberley Valley Winery

TEXAS WINERIES

from the Texas plains came into play again when they made wine flow from the Texas vineyards at the end of the twentieth century. In the 1970s, a handful of individuals tempered that famous Texas pioneer spirit with a little patience and common sense. While the rest of America ran headlong into vineyard expansion, these Texans took a deliberate, methodical approach to planting small test vineyards across the state. These pioneers began laying the groundwork, both in the vineyards and the halls of legislation, for a resurgence of commercial wine production in Texas.

Dr. Bobby Smith, owner of La Buena Vida Winery, is an advocate for Texas wine legislation. In 1977 he was instrumental in the passage of the Farm Winery Act that permitted winemakers to produce and bottle wine in dry counties (counties in which the sale of alcoholic beverages is prohibited) as long as distribution occurred outside of the dry county. This was a giant step for the wineries and growing regions of North Texas.

Ed Auler is another pioneer of Texas wine legislation. He and his wife Susan have played an important part in the marketing of Texas wines. From lobbying for legislation to establishing wine and food festivals, the Auler's continue to play a large part in the growth of the Texas wine industry.

The 1980s saw a dramatic expansion of vineyard acreage and the number of bonded wineries in Texas. Currently, Texas has twenty-seven wineries. (See map for their names and locations.) Interestingly, the average number of bonded wineries has remained fairly constant over the past few decades after reaching a low in the early 1970s. In the late 1980s and in the year 1900, there were over twenty-five wineries in the state.

RECOGNITION FOR TEXAS WINES

Another major advance for the Texas wine industry in the 1980s was the recognition of viticulture areas in Texas. In November 1986, the U.S. government announced the establishment of the Bell Mountain Viticulture Area. This honor recognized the Bell Mountain area of the Texas Hill Country for its ideal soil and climate conditions. It was the first Texas wine-

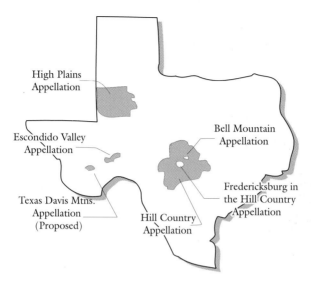

High Plains
Appellation

Escondido Valley
Appellation

Bell Mountain
Appellation

Texas Davis Mtns.
Appellation
(Proposed)

Fredericksburg in
the Hill Country
Appellation

Hill Country
Appellation

TEXAS WINE-GROWING VITICULTURE AREAS

growing appellation and a great addition to Bell Mountain's wine labels. Today there are five viticulture appellation areas— High Plains, Escondido Valley, Hill Country, Bell Mountain, and Fredericksburg in the Hill Country. A sixth, the Davis Mountains Appellation, is pending approval of its application.

LOOKING TOWARD TOMORROW

As we stand on the threshold of a new millennium, wine seems to be playing a more important role in many of our lives. Numerous studies indicate that moderate wine consumption is beneficial when included in a healthy lifestyle. The increase of wine-related activities in Texas, such as festivals, wine seminars, wine society chapters, and vintner dinners, bears witness to the state's desire to become connected to a myriad of elements of Western civilization that for over 8,000 years have maintained wine as a key cultural thread.

In the 1990s, Texas rallied to become the fifth largest wine-producing state in the nation, just behind California, New York,

THE FERMENTING OF WHOLE-BERRY CLUSTERS IS BECOMING INCREASINGLY POPULAR WITH TEXAS WINEMAKERS.
(COURTESY OF THE TEXAS DEPARTMENT OF AGRICULTURE)

Washington, and Oregon. Texas' 1996 production was 1,197,000 gallons from 3,122 acres of wine grapes. Vineyard managers are learning how to apply and adapt the techniques used in the Old World and in California to the unique Texas environment. Where the experts once thought that only hybrid grapes would survive, vinifera varietals are flourishing across the state to produce wines that regularly capture awards in international competitions.

Texas vintners produce a wide array of classic and specialized wines. For red wine lovers there is a very good selection of robust Cabernet Sauvignons with blackberry, vanilla, and toasty flavors; Merlots with a more silky flavor to the palate; Zinfandels with rich, thick, woody, nutmeg flavors; and Pinot Noirs that offer the wine lover a lighter, yet full-bodied wine. White-wine drinkers will appreciate the diverse selection of Chardonnays that range from light and fruity to full, oaken creations that fill the mouth with a buttery explosion. Vintners across the state also offer Sauvignon Blanc, Chenin Blanc, and Muscat Canelli. The German heritage we spoke of earlier is wonderfully showcased in the fine selection of Reisling and Gewurztraminer, especially from the Hill Country wineries.

For those of you who enjoy something out of the ordinary, that famous pioneer spirit has given Texas vintners the courage to experiment with both technique and grape selection. Texas vintners now offer peach wines, a robust selection of Meads, Blush Merlots, and late-harvest, sweet wines. We can expect to see this trend continue into the next century as new wineries and winemakers join the Texas bunch and make their mark on the industry.

TOURING TEXAS WINERIES

Texas is almost a country of its own. In fact, it was an independent republic for almost a decade in the mid-1800s (1836–1845), and it was during that time that Texas acquired the moniker of "The Lone Star State," because of the single star in the republic's flag.

Second only to Alaska in size, Texas offers a landscape that is hard to match. In East Texas you will find over 23 million acres of forest, while in West Texas the rugged Davis Mountains stand with more than 90 peaks over a mile high. South Texas is a water recreation dream with over 600 miles of coastline along the mild Gulf of Mexico. In the vast expanses of the High Plains region of the Panhandle area, it's rumored that on a clear day, you can see all the way up into Canada.

This diverse geography is divided into five wine-grape-growing regions by the Texas Agricultural Department: High Plains, North Central, Trans Pecos, Hill Country, and South Eastern. Each region has a unique climatic, geographic, and cultural character that defines the wines produced within. When it comes to touring Texas wineries, however, the state's infamous size and diversity have proved to be a hindrance in the past. For wine tourists, finding a winery in a state measuring 900 miles from east to west is like trying to find a needle in a haystack.

We have created six wine trails that we believe will put at your fingertips the tools you need to find not only the haystack, but the needles within. These trails are the Munson Trail in north central Texas, the Enchanted Trail and the Highland Trail in the Hill Country, the Brazos Trail in southeastern Texas, and the Palo Duro Trail and the Pecos Trail in West Texas. Each wine

TEXAS WINE TRAILS

trail is your road map to wine tasting and fun in the towns along the trail. The scale of the vineyards and the capacities of the wineries increase as you travel the trails from East to West Texas.

The Munson Trail is in the agricultural area of north central Texas and includes five wineries. The Hill Country, which is assuredly the most romantic area in Texas, is divided into two wine trails: the Enchanted Trail that tours five wineries and the Highland Trails that include stops at six wineries. This area has something for everyone: lakes, rivers, sleepy enclaves, beautiful vistas, and cozy bed and breakfast accommodations. The Hill Country is host to almost fifty percent of the wineries in the state.

In southeast Texas is the Brazos Trail that includes five wineries. Further west are wineries whose scale and grandeur befit the vastness of West Texas. Along the Palo Duro Trail, which includes three wineries, you will encounter the architectural grandeur of Cap* Rock Winery near Lubbock, and along the Pecos Trail, which includes three wineries, is the sprawling 1,000+ acre vineyard of Ste. Genevieve Wines in Fort Stockton.

TOURS AND TASTINGS

The details of winery tours and tastings vary greatly across the state. Many of the wineries established in the late 1970s and early 1980s were built in dry counties. These wineries, especially in the Dallas area, were forced to move their tasting rooms to another county, sometimes many miles from the wine-producing facilities. Because of this, the wineries can offer the public a taste of their wines, but winery tours are either not available, or only available by special arrangements. The majority of the wineries however have tasting rooms located within the wineries themselves and offer tours of their facilities, often with a stop in the vineyard.

We begin our tour in the lush agricultural area north of the Dallas/Ft. Worth area, as we travel along the Munson Trail.

Chapter 2

NORTH CENTRAL
WINERIES

THE MUNSON TRAIL

*T*he ghosts of great winemakers and viticulturists past haunt this region. Many of the early grape pioneers have long been forgotten, but one stands out in these parts: T. V. Munson. This trail—the Munson Trail—has many unique characteristics, beginning with its name. It is the only trail that is not named after a geographical or geological feature in Texas. It is named instead to honor the groundbreaking work done by Munson and the legacy he left for Texas.

In more modern times, this passion for the grape is found in the likes of Dr. Bobby Smith of La Buena Vida Vineyards and Gabe Parker of Homestead Winery. These men, with wineries in dry counties, were pioneers in the resurgence of the Texas wine industry. Both have been active over the decades in working with the Texas legislature to enact laws to keep Texas competitive with other state wine industries. But, more about them later!

We will visit five wineries along this north central trail: Homestead Winery, Hidden Springs Winery, La Buena Vida Winery, Delaney Vineyards, and La Bodega Winery. Another unique characteristic of this trail is the strange mix of wineries represent-

◀ THE WINE INSIDE THESE BARRELS SLOWLY ABSORBS THE CHARACTER OF THE WOOD. (COURTESY OF THE TEXAS DEPARTMENT OF AGRICULTURE)

THE MUNSON TRAIL

🍂 Homestead Vineyard and Winery 🍂 Delaney Vineyards
🍂 Hidden Springs Winery 🍂 La Bodega Winery
🍂 La Buena Vida Winery

---

ed. From a visitor's perspective, they are a collection of off-site tasting rooms, a one-of-a-kind airport winery, and an architectural jewel—a diversity befitting only the Dallas/Ft. Worth area.

The Munson Trail, with its roots in the forest and farmland near Denison, delights the wine tourist by offering quiet, bucolic pastures and loads of history in the many small towns, as well as the beauty and excess of the Dallas/Ft. Worth area. The trail will take you over approximately one-hundred-and-seventy miles of scenic landscapes, and stops at towns such as Denison, Denton, Grapevine, and Dallas. You will also pass through smaller towns such as Whitesboro, Collinsville, Tioga, and Pilot Point.

Using Dallas as our base camp, our first stop is the Homestead Winery tasting room in the town of Denison, seventy-five miles north of Dallas on US 75. Our next stop is Hidden Springs Winery in the town of Pilot Point. Approximately sixty miles north of Dallas, this winery is located on SH 377, in the middle of town. "Just past the Texaco station," as one of the staff told us on the phone—and she was right. It serves as a good landmark. Winemaker Lela Banks, educated at Grayson County College, produces wines that reflect the warmth of her personality. From Hidden Springs Winery, we travel back toward Dallas, to the town of Grapevine, where the unique tasting room of La Buena Vida Winery and the Delaney Vineyards' architectural jewel will be found. Our last stop is Dallas/Ft. Worth Airport (DFW), home to La Bodega Winery—yes, that's right, a winery smack in the middle of an airport terminal!

After enjoying these wineries, we will end our journey in Dallas/Ft. Worth. This metropolis will entice you with culinary delights, incredible shopping excursions, stockyards, fine arts, theater, museums, and subtle (and not-so-subtle) entertainment spots. Local restaurants are also big supporters of Texas wines. Be sure to ask for them.

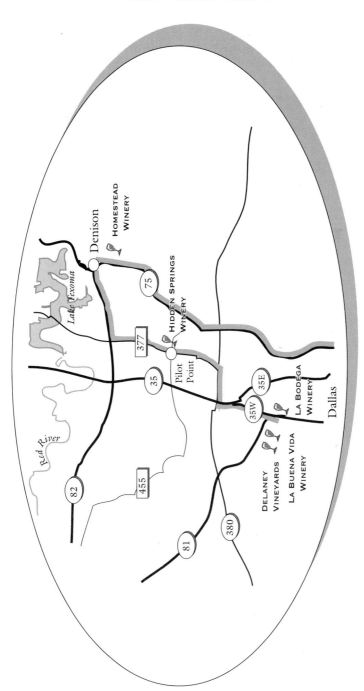

THE MUNSON TRAIL WINERIES

We begin our tour with Homestead Winery in one of two ways. If you're a Type-A personality who "just likes to get there already," then heading north on US-75 is the way to go. If one the other hand, you would like to take a backroad to Denison, even though it will take slightly longer, try SH 289, which parallels IH-75, about eleven miles to the west. SH 289 delights the traveler with sights and sounds of small towns like Frisco, Prosper, and Gunter. Please note: The tasting room in Denison was scheduled to open in the summer of 1998. Call the winery for the status of their progress.

Once in downtown Denison, you can find Homestead Wineries' tasting room on Main Street. A little warning for you, plan on spending more time than you may have thought in Denison. The people and atmosphere will make you want to linger to take in all the historic sites and sample some of the food and shopping available.

❧Homestead Vineyards and Winery

Winery: P.O. Box 35, Ivanhoe, Texas 75447

Phone (903) 583-4281

Homestead Winery is a small, boutique-style family operation located on the grounds of the Parker Homestead, which gives the winery its name. Because the winery is located in a dry county, however, the owners will open a tasting room in historic downtown Denison in the summer of 1998.

Gabe and Barbara Parker came to winemaking from a heritage that includes more than 100 years of farming in North Texas. This gives the family a level of expertise unmatched by other grape growers in the area. Gabe is a rancher, businessman, and

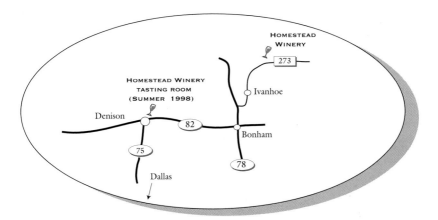

HOMESTEAD VINEYARDS AND WINERY

farmer. After spending years in the corporate world, he decided to go back to his roots and started his vineyard in 1983.

The winery was bonded in 1989 and with the help of wine consultant Roy Mitchell has grown consistently, and in 1996 produced 3,000 cases of wine. Gabe's heritage in farming quickly helped him establish a robust vineyard and made the Homestead name a label of quality and distinctive wines.

The winery has intentionally been kept small over the years, which allows greater control of the winemaking process. Gabe's philosophy is simple: The quality of the wine starts with the quality of the vineyard. Gabe feels that the awards his wines continue to win are the results of the skill of his winemaker and the quality of his grapes.

Gabe's efforts in defining and enhancing the Texas wine industry have led him, like Bobby Smith of La Buena Vida Winery, to be a catalyst for new legislation to help the wine industry flourish in the state. He also assists with a variety of festivals to promote the industry in this and other areas of the state.

THE WINES

Roy Mitchell is Homestead's winemaker and is well-known in the Texas wine industry. A pioneer of the early 1970s research in grape production, Dr. Mitchell helped to establish the first new commercial winery in Texas—Llano Estacado. He has been a consultant to numerous wineries in the state and has assisted growers with grape production problems. Roy knows how to grow grapes in Texas, perhaps better than anyone. He brings a classic sense of winemaking to Homestead Winery, and working with Gabe, produces blended wines with grapes picked from the Homestead Vineyard and vineyards around the state. Some of Homestead's most popular wines include Muscat Canelli, Roses of Ivanhoe, Cabernet Sauvignon, and Chardonnay, all of which enjoy distribution across a large area of Texas. Gabe is especially proud of the success of his Muscat Canelli. It was one of the first wines ever produced in this area of Texas.

DIRECTIONS: AFTER TOURING HOMESTEAD WINERY, WE WILL TURN WESTWARD ON SH 82 FOR APPROXIMATELY EIGHTEEN MILES. TURNING SOUTH ON SH 377, IT IS A SHORT TRIP TO THE TOWN OF PILOT POINT AND HIDDEN SPRINGS WINERY.

♣Hidden Springs Winery

256 North Highway 377, Pilot Point, Texas 76273
(817) 665-8177

OPEN: 10 A.M.–6 P.M.
TUESDAY–SATURDAY;
1–6 P.M. SUNDAY

TOURS, TASTINGS,
RETAIL SALES, AND GIFTS

Turning onto SH 380, you will probably breathe a sigh of contentment as you travel through this north Texas agricultural area. The roadsides are awash in green, be it from untouched trees or the meticulously planted fields of the local farmers' vegetables. The fast pace of big-city life is far behind you and the tranquil agricultural area will have a calming effect, putting you in just the right mood for Hidden Springs Winery.

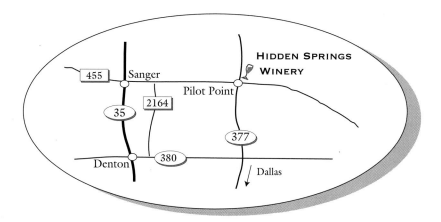

HIDDEN SPRINGS WINERY

This unassuming facility, which looks like a remodeled office building from the road, is full of Victorian charm and elegance. You know in the back of your mind that you just turned off a busy highway, and you are also vaguely aware that in the backrooms of this winery, people are feverishly working on setting up a private party or bottling this year's new crush, but it doesn't seem to matter. Jim and Lela Banks, along with the wonderful staff working with them, have cleverly created a remarkably calm and friendly environment in which to sample their wines.

Lela Banks, winemaker and co-owner, had been an amateur winemaker for years prior to her formal education at Grayson County College in the early 1990s. She was awarded a scholarship at Clos du Vougeot in France to complete her studies for an Associate of Applied Science in Viticulture and Enology. The vineyard in Whitesboro had been in existence long before the opening of Hidden Springs Winery. In fact, the winery owes its name to the springs located on the property. As Lela tells it, when she and her husband purchased the property, they were told that it had a number of natural springs. During excursions on the property their first year, they managed to find three springs, but were told by neighbors that there was a fourth.

After moving in, Lela and Jim noticed that a car would often drive slowly by their home, but never stop. Finally, when Lela was in the front yard one day, the driver, an elderly woman, stopped to talk. As the conversation went on, Lela learned that this woman was part of the original family that started the farm, and she knew exactly where that last "hidden" spring was located. After finding what turned out to be the prettiest of the springs, according to Lela, they decided that Hidden Springs would be the name of their yet-to-be-formed winery.

The winery is located in a building that has gone through many reincarnations: an office, a restaurant, and even a honky-tonk saloon. After extensive remodeling, the Bankses have created a comfortable atmosphere filled with antiques from Europe. The tasting room features a massive turn-of-the-century bar from a Texas saloon, backed by a marble credenza surrounded by oversized walnut-framed mirrors. The magnificent chandelier is festooned with over 300 lead-crystal drops.

After sampling their wines, you may embark on a tour of the winery facilities by passing through a gothic-styled solid-oak door brought here from an Austrian wine cellar. The tour culminates with a pass through the function room and the gift shop, both well appointed in the Victorian theme. The function room is available for wedding receptions, teas, luncheons, corporate functions, and other special events. The gift shop is a comfortable unpretentious display of food items intermixed with arts and crafts of some fine Texas artists.

THE UNMISTAKABLE SIGN FOR HIDDEN SPRINGS WINERY.

During the time of our visit, Jim and Lela had just celebrated the winery's first anniversary on July 4th. Keep that date in mind when you plan a trip to this winery. A multi-day celebration is usually planned with food, music, and of course, wine. If the wines Lela has created in this first year are any indicator, Hidden Springs Winery has a long, successful future in front of it. At a current production capacity of 4,000 gallons, their first goal is to be able to handle larger quantities. Expansion will include acquiring 10,000 gallon tanks, which should allow them to have their wine available in the Denison and Dallas areas.

THE WINES

Hidden Springs is a young winery, though you couldn't tell that by tasting the wines. Opened in 1996 on the Fourth of July, it offers a good range of red and white wines. Though somewhat guarded about her winemaking techniques, Lela admits that she prefers making "lighter" wines. She uses stainless-steel fermentation for her whites, even the Chardonnay that she only "ran the roots of the oak tree through." The Chardonnay is a light, fruity creation, quite different from the oakey, buttery wines that are created by barrel fermentation. Lela also prefers just a little oak fermentation for her reds to avoid a heavy tannin flavor. When she does use oak, Lela uses both French and American oak at Hidden Springs, but prefers the flavor of the French.

With only eighteen acres of their own grapes, the Bankses must rely on vineyards from other areas of the state to supplement a growing demand for their wine. This has forced Lela to be a more creative winemaker, in that she does a large amount of blending for her wines. Her Ruby Glow, a particular favorite of ours during our visit, is a blend of eighty percent Ruby Cabernet, ten percent Cabernet Franc, five percent Cabernet Sauvignon, and five percent Merlot. This blend produces a nice smooth taste, with just a hint of a tannin aftertaste to fill out the mouth. A similar blending experiment—the Crystal Red—is a mixture of fifty percent Cabernet Sauvignon, twenty percent Mixed Red (it's a secret!), fifteen percent Cabernet Franc, twelve percent Ruby Cabernet, and three percent Merlot. We won't tell you about this one; you'll have to taste it for yourself.

THE QUALITY WINES OF HIDDEN SPRINGS WINERY.

Lela plans to experiment with Merlot—as a Merlot. Today she uses Merlot as a blending wine, feeling over the years that it lacked enough of a presence to stand on its own. However, she is a pragmatist, and noting Merlot's popularity in the market, will honor the wishes of her customers. A good-natured individual with a quick smile, Lela brings a strong sense of professionalism to her craft. In her words, "Nothing will go behind our label that is not quality and consistent." Therefore, if this winemaker—who likes to wear red socks when making red wines and white socks when making white wines—decides to release a Merlot, you can bet it will be her best.

Aware of the importance of marketing, the Bankses will also experiment with different label concepts. Look for them to use glass etching on their bottles, a process that carves a design into the glass. They also will offer private labeling of their wines, a service that is seeing a sharp rise in popularity in the 1990s. Plans for the facility also include the construction of a romantic Victorian gazebo and a small vineyard.

When you buy their wines, the staff will ask if you would like the optional gift-wrap service they offer. We suggest you have at least one bottle wrapped this way. They do a wonderful job! The wrapping was so attractive, in fact, that two of the three bottles we had wrapped, never made it out of Dallas. Friends we visited saw the bottles and just had to have them. While we hated to part with Lela's wine, we were happy to introduce our friends to delicious Texas wine.

DIRECTIONS: FROM HIDDEN SPRINGS WINERY, WE WILL BACKTRACK TO DALLAS ALONG IH-35, TAKING IH-35W AS WE NEAR DALLAS, THEN HEAD EAST ON SH 114 INTO THE HISTORIC TOWN OF GRAPEVINE TO VISIT LA BUENA VIDA WINERY.

♣La Buena Vida Winery

416 East College Street, Grapevine, Texas 76135
Phone (817) 329-3145

OPEN: MONDAY–SATURDAY
10 A.M.–5 P.M.
SUNDAY 12–5 P.M.

TOURS, TASTINGS,
RETAIL SALES, AND GIFTS
$5 FOR A TASTING

Welcome to La Buena Vida Winery in Grapevine, Texas. In the Texas wine industry, historic Grapevine is akin to sacred ground. Town fathers requested, and received, special legislation that allows wineries to sell wine by the glass for consumption on the premises in counties designated as wet counties.

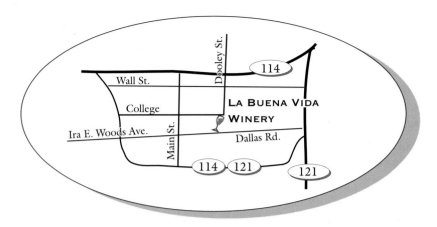

LA BUENA VIDA WINERY

It is fitting then, that Dr. Bobby Smith, owner of La Buena Vida, decided to move his tasting room to Grapevine since he was a key promoter of the Farm Winery Act of 1977. This bill permits winemakers to produce wine in a dry county, as long as it is sold in a wet county. A secondary, but no less important benefit of this legislation, was that it opened the doors for the creation of small wineries across the state of Texas.

This small family-owned winery, the first to establish a tasting room in Grapevine, has been making wine since the early '70s. It is the third-oldest winery in Texas and the first in the north-eastern section of the state. It is also the last of three wineries originally established in Parker County.

Bob and his son Steve, the winemaker for La Buena Vida, produce wines under three separate labels: Springtown, Smith Estates, and Walnut Creek. The Springtown label includes Sauvignon Blanc, Springtown Rain (a white table wine), and Springtown Mist (a blush wine). The Smith Estate label is reserved for their champagnes. A special label, the Texmas Blush, a wine released for Christmas is a particular favorite with visitors.

Eager to participate in the Grapevine concept, Bobby purchased an abandoned church on College Street, smack in the middle of a residential neighborhood. After extensive remodeling, the tasting room opened its doors in mid-1995, and Grapevine has not been the same since. Development continues to this day as Bobby enhances the grounds around the building with greenery, shady arbors, fountains, herb gardens, and a beautiful adjoining patio area for special functions.

We met Bobby on a recent visit to the tasting room. At an age when most men would prefer a leisurely round of golf or a cigar with the guys, Bobby was out back driving posts, stringing trellis wire, and planting vines in 90° plus heat. He is developing an experimental vineyard on the property to produce Grapevine select wines.

Bobby told us that it has been somewhat of an uphill battle to bring the wine industry back to this part of Texas, but he has had plenty of help over the years convincing legislatures. Humbly, he is quick to point out that it took the efforts of much more than one man to bring about the needed changes, and he is happy to participate in the Grapevine concept.

LA BUENA VIDA WINERY TASTING ROOM.

Camille McBee has been with the winery from its early days and is responsible for public relations for the winery, managing special events and corporate functions, and deftly organizing the winery's participation in various festivals and competitions.

Her effervescence and enthusiasm is infectious as she discusses the winery and its participation in the city of Grapevine. Camille sees La Buena Vida as unique in that it fills a "niche" market in the industry. This winery is truly one of the experimental wineries in the state. Releasing wines under three labels: Springtown, Smith Estates, and Walnut Creek, La Buena Vida creates a selection of wines that is a unique mixture of table wines, traditional varietals, and dessert and specialized wines.

THE WINES

Under the Springtown label you will find Springtown Red, Springtown Rain, and Springtown Mist, all light, fruity wines with wonderful aromatics. The Smith Estates label is reserved for their line of champagnes—La Buena Vida was one of the first Texas wineries to offer champagnes. The Walnut Creek label is used for La Buena Vida's vintage Port, which has been the winery's most decorated wine over the years.

The Smiths produce their wines from a combination of grapes from their Springtown vineyard and other vineyards around Texas. They plan to expand their twenty-five-acre vineyard by five acres a year, which may not seem ambitious, but considering the effort required for trellis, irrigation, and the vines themselves, it is quite a task to undertake. The existing vineyard is a mixture of grapes including Chambourcin, Chenin Blanc, Riesling, Pinot Noir, and Pinot Blanc. Camille expects to see something special from the Pinot Blanc in two to three years.

A special label, the Texmas Blush, a wine released for Christmas, is a particular favorite with visitors. The label features Santa and reindeer—from a Texas perspective—along with a slightly modified version of "The Night Before Christmas." Another favorite during the holiday season is the Scarborough Mead, a spiced wine best served heated. This particular wine has been an award-winner from its inception, as has its attractive label, the latest version of which includes caricatures of those responsible for passing the important legislation in Grapevine.

The future holds excitement and promise for La Buena Vida. The Smiths will soon feature new wines, including a Merlot Elegance, which will be a dry blush, and a wine they will call Poure Elegance, which at fourteen percent alcohol, will be a pear-based dessert wine.

Something even more exciting than the new provocative-sounding wines next year is the importation of Merlot and Chardonnay bulk juice from Chile. The scarcity of grapes and grape juice in America is forcing many winemakers around the country to look for alternative sources. Because of weather conditions and the fact that Pierce's disease reduced tonnage in 1996, Texas vintners have been forced to be creative for future production. With Bobby and Steve at the helm, however, expect more inventive and marvelous wines coming from this winery.

DEVELOPMENT IN GRAPEVINE

To complement the groundbreaking work planned in the wineries around town, the city of Grapevine is also planning some exciting changes. The city has grown dramatically from a sleepy town of a decade ago to a major tourist stop between Dallas and Ft. Worth. Numerous shops, restaurants, hotels, and historic buildings will capture your imagination, the Grand Old Opry will make you dance, and Grapevine Mills will offer you an incredible shopping experience found in only a handful of places around America. For you train buffs, the historic, steam-driven Tarantula Train will take you from the restored train station in Grapevine to downtown Ft. Worth. If you happen to be staying in Ft. Worth, this train is a convenient way to take an excursion to the Grapevine wineries.

DIRECTIONS: FROM OUR VISIT TO LA BUENA VIDA WINERY, WE TAKE A SHORT TRIP WEST ALONG SH 114 TO SH 121, THEN SOUTH TO GLADE RD. TO VISIT THE ARCHITECTURAL DELIGHT THAT IS DELANEY VINEYARDS.

❧Delaney Vineyards

2000 Champagne, Grapevine, Texas 76051

Phone (817) 481-5668 Fax: (817) 251-8119

OPEN: 10 A.M.–5 P.M.
TUESDAY–SATURDAY;
12–5 P.M. SUNDAY

TOURS, TASTINGS,
RETAIL SALES, AND GIFTS
$5 FOR A TASTING;
$7 FOR A TOUR

Since opening in 1995, the Delaney winery along SH 121 has already become a landmark for folks living in the area. Fashioned after an eighteen-century French winery, the magnificent structure is surrounded by a century-old stand of oak trees and a lush, ten-acre vineyard. Passersby could easily mistake this site for a European winery on a picture postcard.

Passing through the massive doors of the winery, you are swept back in time to the Renaissance period by the hand-painted frescos that adorn the vaulted ceiling of the entry. The masterful paintings incorporate

DELANEY VINEYARD'S ATTENTION TO DETAIL IS EVEN EVIDENT IN THE WINERY'S WOODWORK.

THE EUROPEAN AMBIANCE OF DELANEY VINEYARDS.

images of cherubs, who supposedly guard the winery from evil at night. Once inside the winery, the eighteen-inch thick walls block out all outside sounds, as a winery greeter points you toward the well-appointed gift shop where you are encouraged to browse through their wines and gifts while you wait for the next tour to begin.

A tour through the facility gives you a better appreciation of the meticulous planning that went into the design and construction of this facility. Owners Jerry and Linda Delaney, toured wineries across France for a number of years to help them incorporate the essential elements of a grand French winery. A bell tower chime, set at a volume that will not disturb the neighbors, is their attempt to capture the atmosphere of a winery in a small village of France.

The tour finishes in the Barrel Room, which contains a generous 5,000 square feet and seems even larger as you look upward at the soaring vaulted ceiling. The massive stacks of American and French oak fermenting barrels are themselves dwarfed by the shear size of this room. At the far end is the tasting bar that is attended by the well-educated staff who will assist you with a wine tasting.

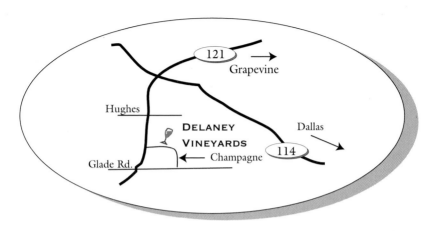

DELANEY VINEYARDS

THE WINES

Delaney uses grapes from the ten-acre vineyard that surrounds the winery as well as grapes from their seventy-eight-acre vineyard near Lamesa, Texas, which was established in 1987. Wine is produced at both the Lamesa and Grapevine wineries using a combination of stainless-steel tanks and oak barrels to achieve the proper fermentation qualities, depending on the variety.

The 1994 Cabernet Sauvignon, a blend of Cabernet Sauvignon, Merlot, and Cabernet Franc, was produced following the traditional Bordeaux methods, using egg whites for finning, or clarifying, the wine prior to bottling. After more than fifteen months of oak aging, the wine has a delicate bouquet with cherry undertones. The Delaneys expect this wine to continue to age in the bottle over the next ten years. The 1995 Cabernet Sauvignon bears the distinction of having been completely produced in French oak.

Between these bursts of wine activity, the Barrel Room plays host to a number of catered events and private parties and has had the honor of hosting numerous weddings. Jerry and Linda continuously expand the events in this facility. In 1997, the room served as a backdrop for filming a series of perfume commercials. Look for more creative happenings over the next few years.

The 1996 barrel-fermented Chardonnay, made with Chardonnay grapes from the Delaney's High Plains vineyards was fermented to dryness in French oak and matured "surlies," sediment at the bottom of the fermentation vessel. It possesses a soft creamy taste with a buttery bouquet, which would go well with seafood and cheeses.

Delaney Vineyards also produce a Texas Rose Blush wine that is a combination of Chardonnay and Cabernet Franc. Promoted as a good summer red wine, it is sweet enough to almost be a dessert wine and good with barbecue. Their Texas White table wine, on the other hand—a combination of Chardonnay and Sauvignon Blanc—has a spicy, nutmeg flavor, and is good for picnics. Under the watchful hand of French winemaster Jacques Recht, Delaney Vineyards also offer a Merlot, Riesling, Pinot Noir, and a Zinfandel.

THE WINES OF DELANEY VINEYARDS AGING IN FRENCH OAK.

DIRECTIONS: OUR TRAIL WILL CONCLUDE WITH A VISIT TO THE ONLY WINERY IN AN AIRPORT: LA BODEGA WINERY IN DFW. WE WILL TRAVEL ON SH 121 TO SH 114 AND HEAD EAST TOWARD THE AIRPORT. THE WINERY IS LOCATED IN TERMINAL 2-E, GATE 6.

La Bodega Winery

Terminal 2-E, Dallas/Ft. Worth Airport

P.O. Box 100, Grapevine, Texas 76099

Phone (817) 329-3145

OPEN: 10 A.M.–5 P.M. MONDAY–SATURDAY; 12–5 P.M. SUNDAY
TASTINGS, RETAIL SALES, AND GIFTS
$5 FOR A TASTING

A winery in an airport? Yes, welcome to the world's first and only (as far as we know) bonded winery to be located in an airport. Located within the city limits of Grapevine, the DFW Airport is included in the legislation that makes Grapevine attractive to wineries.

A visit to La Bodega is just plain fun. The hustle and bustle of the airport terminal, with people off to strange (or not-so-strange lands), serves as an exciting backdrop for this small niche of space carved into Terminal 2-E. While it is a real bonded winery, La Bodega is at present a small tasting room that features La Bodega's wines and more than thirty Texas wines from across the state.

Gina Puente, owner of La Bodega explains that initially she produced her wines by using the facilities of a nearby Texas winery, while she developed a small facility of her own within the airport tasting room.

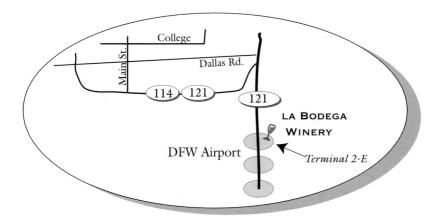

LA BODEGA WINERY

Despite the lack of a vineyard and traditional stainless-steel vats and oak barrels one expects to see at a winery, Gina and her staff have created a warm, inviting area to sit and sample Texas wines. Just a step away from the river of humans and transport carts that whiz by, we found ourselves lingering by the tasting bar longer than we had anticipated. There is something infectious about the place—something about relaxing and sipping a glass of wine as the world seems to rush by.

THE WINES

La Bodega offers a limited number of wines under their label: Cabernet Sauvignon, Chardonnay, and a selection of table wines. When we spoke with Gina, she was enthusiastic about the future for the winery over the next few years. She connected the tasting room to her newsstand next door by using a cave-like passageway between the two retail spaces. This connection allows customers to move freely between the two stores while maintaining the ambiance of the tasting room. The tasting room offers fast turnaround on custom and personal labels for corporations, groups, and individuals.

La Bodega will soon feature guest appearances of Texas winemakers for bottle signings and tastings to highlight different

LA BODEGA WINERY OFFERS YOU A CALM PLACE IN THE HECTIC AIRPORT TERMINAL.

Texas wineries. The Texas wine industry is excited about this cutting-edge approach of placing a winery within an airport. Gina's efforts are being praised for introducing more people to Texas wines and wineries.

ALONG THE TRAIL

The Munson Trail winds through a rich patchwork of forests and grassland that offers farming, ranching, winegrowing, as well as the charisma of small towns and the excitement of a major metropolis in America. Quite a mixture, wouldn't you say?

What exactly does this mean to you? For starters it means that by traveling along the Munson Trail you will experience some of the best scenery and will meet some of the friendliest people in Texas. Take Denison, Texas, for example. Just spitting distance from the Red River, Denison is a place where folks know each other by name on the streets and are likely to say hello to you even though you're a stranger. Folks here are cordial, so please, say hello in return! And here's a tip for you city folks—when an approaching driver waves to you, wave back—it's only neighborly.

Further south, the land is filled with the trademarks of Texas: horses and cattle. Horse ranches dominate your trip back toward Dallas, and Fort Worth is proud of its stockyard heritage. But Fort Worth is much more than stockyards these days: museums, water gardens, restaurants—the city is more than capable of surviving in the shadow of Dallas. Then there's Dallas! Immortalized by oil, the Dallas Cowboys, and J. R. Ewing, like many other major American cities, you either love it or hate it. Yes, Dallas is a modern behemoth of glistening skyscrapers, but it also has a softer side. Dallas is also about Victorian homes, tree-lined streets, wonderful restaurants, nightclubs, and fashion. Dallas has—dare we say—areas that will simply charm you! Stay at the Stoneleigh Hotel for a weekend and explore the area—you'll see what we mean.

Finally, nestled between Dallas and Ft. Worth, in the shadow of DFW Airport, is the historic town of Grapevine. From our perspective, the outstanding efforts that city fathers have made to bring the wine industry to the forefront of tourism in the area has given Grapevine a new focus. It seems that in every season, Grapevine has a wine-related event, whether it's the Texas New Vintage Wine and Food Festival in April, Main Street Days in May, Grapefest in September, or the Christmas Parade of Lights in December. Grapevine also has plenty to offer in terms of history, food, shopping, and the famous Tarantula Steam Train that provides rides between Grapevine and Fort Worth.

With all that the communities along this trail have to offer, you might want to give yourself a few extra days to enjoy the wineries and the sights and sounds along the way.

Bed and Breakfasts Along the Munson Trail

Denison

IVY BLUE

Hosts: Lane and Tammy Segerstrom, 1100 W. Sears, Denison 75020, (888) IVY-BLUE, (903) 463-2479, fax (903) 465-6773, 4 guest rooms, 4 baths, Carriage House (2 suites), Garden House (1 suite), gourmet breakfast, $$, children only in Carriage House, no pets, smoking on designated areas outside, MC, V, AE, D

THE MOLLY CHERRY

Hosts: Regina and Jim Widener, 200 Molly Cherry Lane, Denison 75020, (903) 465-0575, 1 suite, 2 guest rooms, 2 baths, 4 suites in 2 hideaway cottages, full breakfast, $$–$$$$, no pets, designated smoking areas, all cr

Denton

GODFREY'S PLACE INN

Hosts: Marjorie and Dick Waters, 1513 N. Locust, Denton 76201, (940) 381-1118, fax (940) 566-0856, or Bed & Breakfast Texas Style (972) 298-8586, 4 guest rooms, 4 baths, heart-healthy gourmet breakfast, $$–$$$, no children, no pets, no smoking, MC, V

Dallas

AMERICAN DREAM B&B

Hosts: Pat and Andre, P.O. Box 670275, Dallas 75367, (800) 373-2690 or (214) 356-6536, fax (214) 357-9034, 2 suites, gourmet breakfast, $$, children by special arrangement, no pets, smoking only on patio, MC, V

COURTYARD ON THE TRAIL

Host: Alan Kagan, (972) 553-9700, or contact Bed & Breakfast Texas Style, (972) 298-8586, 2 guest rooms, 2 baths, full breakfast, $$$, no children, no pets, no smoking, MC, V

THE CLOISTERS

Contact Bed & Breakfast Texas Style, (972) 298-8586, 2 guest rooms, 2 baths, full breakfast, $$, no children, no pets, smoking outdoors only, MC, V

Fort Worth

AZALEA PLANTATION

Innkeepers: Martha and Richard Linnartz, 1400 Robinwood Dr., Fort Worth 76111, (800) 68-RELAX, (817) 838-5882, 2 guest rooms, 2 baths, 1 cottage with 2 suites, full breakfast buffet style (weekends), continental plus (weekdays), $$–$$$, no pets, outside smoking only, MC, V, AE, D

ETTA'S PLACE

Hosts: Bonnie and Vaughn Franks, 200 W. Third St., Fort Worth 76102, (817) 654-0267, fax (817) 878-2560, 4 suites, 6 rooms, choice of continental or full breakfast, $$$–$$$$, children and pets welcome, smoking on balconies, all cr

MISS MOLLY'S HOTEL

Host: Mark Hancock, 109½ West Exchange Avenue, Fort Worth 76106, (800) 996-6559, (817) 626-1522, fax (817) 625-2723, 8 rooms, 4 baths, continental plus breakfast, $–$$$, no pets or smokers, MC, V

THE TEXAS WHITE HOUSE

Hosts: Grover and Jamie McMains, 1417 Eighth Ave., Fort Worth 76104, (800) 279-6491, (817) 923-3597, fax (817) 923-0410, 3 guest rooms, 3 baths, gourmet breakfast, $$–$$$, no children, no pets, smoking on front porch, MC, V, AE, D

Grapevine

THE 1934 BED AND BREAKFAST

322 E. College St., Grapevine 76051, (817) 251-1934, 3 guest rooms, Motor Car Room for meetings and receptions, 5-course gourmet breakfast, $$$–$$$$

RESTAURANTS ALONG THE MUNSON TRAIL

Denison

THE POINT RESTAURANT AND CLUB

On Lake Texoma (take US 75 north to FM 84, then west about 10 miles and follow signs), Denison, (903) 475-6376, Steak and seafood, breakfast on Saturday and Sunday, Bar, $$

Denton

LOCUST ST. GRILL

104 N Locust, (940) 566-3614, Denton. Burgers, Steaks, Seafood, Pasta. Bar. Open daily, $$

RICK'S AMERICAN CYBER GRILL

501 W University Dr. @ Carroll, Denton, (940) 382-8260, http://www.cybergrill.com. Burgers and Steaks. Bar. Open daily, $$

TWO BROTHERS ITALIAN RESTAURANT

1125 E University, Denton. (940) 591-9215. Italian. Bar. Texas wines. Open Monday–Saturday, $$

Dallas

ADELMO'S RISTORANTE

4537 Cole Avenue at Knox, Dallas. (214) 559-0325. Italian bistro. Bar. Texas wines. Lunch and dinner Monday–Friday, dinner only on Saturday, $$

ALESSIO'S

4117 Lomo Alto, Dallas, (214) 521-3585. Italian. Semi-formal dress requested. Bar. Texas wines. Lunch Monday–Friday, dinner daily, $$–$$$

ANTARES

300 Reunion Blvd. in Reunion Tower, Dallas, (214) 712-7145. American. Bar. Texas wines. Lunch Monday–Saturday, Sunday brunch, dinner daily, $$

CHEZ GERARD

4444 McKinney at Armstrong, Dallas, (214) 522-6865. French bistro. Bar, Texas wines. Lunch Monday–Friday, dinner Monday–Saturday, $$–$$$

DEL FRISCO'S DOUBLE EAGLE STEAKHOUSE

5251 Spring Valley Road, Dallas, (972) 490-9000. Steak. Bar. Texas wines. Dinner Monday–Saturday, $$–$$$

THE FRENCH ROOM

1321 Commerce Street at Akard in The Adolphus Hotel, Dallas, (214) 742-8200. Bar. Texas wines. Dinner Monday–Saturday, closed Sunday, reservations required, $$$

PAN-SEARED BEEF TENDERLOIN SERVED WITH A SHALLOT TART IN BASIL CABERNET SAUCE IS JUST ONE MENU CHOICE THAT MAKES THE FRENCH ROOM AT THE ADOLPHUS HOTEL A AAA FIVE-DIAMOND RESTAURANT.

LA TRATTORIA LOMBARDI

2916 North Hall Street near McKinney Avenue, Dallas (214) 954-0803. Italian, Bar. Texas wines. Lunch Monday–Friday, dinner seven days, $$–$$$

LOCATED INSIDE A SMALL, LUXURY HOTEL, THE MANSION ON TURTLE CREEK IS THE ONLY RESTAURANT IN TEXAS TO CONSISTENTLY EARN A FIVE-STAR RATING FROM MOBIL AND A FIVE-DIAMOND RATING FROM AAA.

THE MANSION ON TURTLE CREEK

2821 Turtle Creek Blvd. inside The Mansion on Turtle Creek Hotel, (214) 559-2100 or (800) 527-5432. Continental. Bar. Texas wines. Lunch and dinner seven days, Reservations required, $$$

STAR CANYON RESTAURANT

3102 Oak Lawn in The Centrum at Cedar Springs, Dallas, (214) 520-STAR (520-7827). Texas cuisine. Bar. Texas wines. Lunch Monday–Friday, dinner seven days, Reservations required, $$$

STAR CANYON'S BONE-IN COWBOY RIBEYE WITH RED CHILE ONION RINGS IS A STAR EXAMPLE OF CHEF STEPHAN PYLES NEW TEXAS CUISINE.

Fort Worth

THE BALCONY OF RIDGLEA

6100 Bowie Blvd. at Winthrop, Fort Worth, (817) 731-3719. Continental. Bar. Texas wines. Lunch Monday–Friday, dinner Monday–Saturday, closed Sunday, $$

CAFÉ ASPEN RESTAURANT AND BAR

6103 Camp Bowie Blvd., Fort Worth, (817) 738-0838. American. Bar. Texas wines. Lunch and dinner Monday–Saturday, $$

CATTLEMEN'S STEAKHOUSE

2458 North Main in the Stockyards, Fort Worth, (817) 624-3945. Steaks and seafood. Bar. Texas wines. Lunch and dinner seven days, $–$$

CELEBRATION

4600 Dexter Avenue at Camp Bowie and Hulen, (817) 731-6272. American. Bar. Texas wines. Lunch and dinner seven days, $–$$

JOE T. GARCIA'S MEXICAN DISHES

2201 North Commerce near the Stockyards, Fort Worth, (817) 626-4356. Mexican. Bar. Texas wines. Lunch and dinner seven days, $–$$

REFLECTIONS

200 Main Street in The Worthington Hotel, Fort Worth, (817) 882-1765, American and French. Bar. Texas wines. Dinner Monday–Saturday, $$$

REATA

500 Throckmorton Street, Bank One Tower Building, (817) 336-1009. Steak, seafood, Tex-Mex. Bar. Texas wines. Lunch and dinner Monday–Saturday, $–$$

Chapter 3

HILL COUNTRY WINERIES

*I*magine a two-lane road twisting and turning through a valley of shrub-covered limestone hills. Now visualize sparkling lakes nestled in these valleys, slow-moving rivers, fields of wildflowers, and communities rich in German heritage. Welcome to the Texas Hill Country. Welcome to Texas' largest concentration of wineries and holiday destinations. A rich mixture of people, culture, and landscape, this picturesque area serves as the backdrop for the most exciting and romantic wine trails the state has to offer. Once a land of cultural and geological clashes, the Hill Country today is a vibrant viticultural area where past diversities contribute to the character of the region's wine.

THE TRAILS

The Hill Country wineries are found along two trails: the Enchanted Trail and the Highland Trail. We use the city of Austin, Texas' state capital, as the starting point. The Enchanted Trail offers wine tourists an exciting tour of five very distinctive wineries along with an overnight stay in the town of Fredericksburg—always a welcome treat. The Highland Trail, with six wineries, offers magnificent views of the Highland Lakes as you cruise the twisting, turning roads that connect the wineries and returns to Austin for a visit to Cana Cellars Winery.

◀ HARVEST TIME IN A TEXAS VINEYARD IS STILL A LABOR OF LOVE.
(COURTESY OF GRAPE CREEK VINEYARDS)

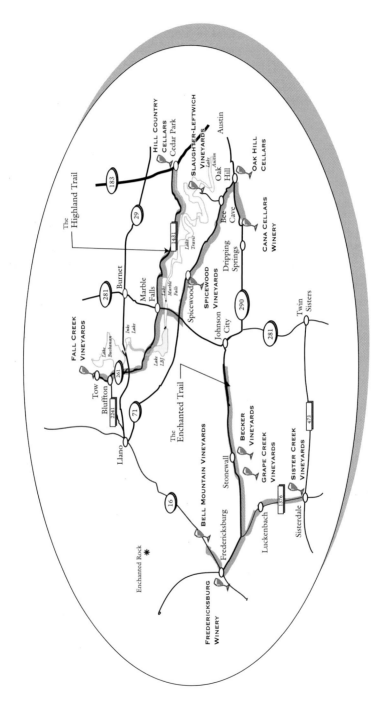

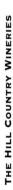

THE HILL COUNTRY WINERIES

THE ENCHANTED TRAIL	THE HIGHLAND TRAIL
✿ Becker Vineyards	✿ Hill Country Cellars
✿ Grape Creek Vineyards	✿ Fall Creek Vineyards
✿ Bell Mountain Vineyards	✿ Spicewood Vineyards
✿ Fredericksburg Winery	✿ Slaughter-Leftwich Vineyards
✿ Sister Creek Vineyards	✿ Cana Cellars Winery
	✿ Oak Hill Cellars

THE ENCHANTED TRAIL WINERIES

Tall cedars, stubby pines, peach orchards, and Old-World-style towns dominate our weekend trip along the Enchanted Trail. This ambitious trail is named for Enchanted Rock State Park located just north of Fredericksburg and will take us to five wineries. The five wineries are Becker Vineyards, Grape Creek Vineyards, Bell Mountain Vineyards, Fredericksburg Winery, and Sister Creek Vineyards.

Our first stop, after leaving Austin, is the town of Stonewall, just east of Fredericksburg on SH 290, and home to both the newly formed Becker Vineyards and the long-established Grape Creek Vineyards. From there we drive directly to Fredericksburg to visit Bell Mountain Vineyards, located on the slopes of Bell Mountain, 14 miles north of town.

You may want to stay overnight in Fredericksburg, and stroll among the antique and specialty shops and restaurants that line Main Street. With a strong German heritage, this town offers a variety of German restaurants and bakeries to tempt even the strongest willpower. Fredericksburg is also a pure delight for lodging, with the largest concentration of bed and breakfasts in Texas. Visitors may choose from more than one hundred beautifully decorated bed and breakfast accommodations, ranging from the traditional (a room in a large home) to Sunday houses and rustic log cabins. For a preview of what is offered, call ahead for a copy of the Fredericksburg Visitor's Guide: 830-997-2155.

Before leaving Fredericksburg, we will visit the Fredericksburg Winery. When we leave this historic German enclave, our trail continues to Sister Creek Vineyards in the small town of Sisterdale. Let's begin our tour!

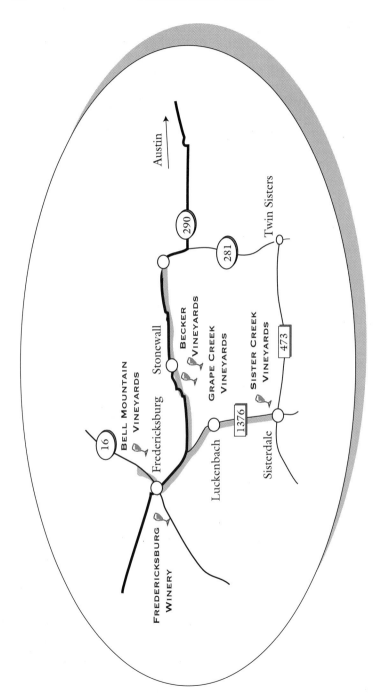

Austin

290

281

Twin Sisters

473

BECKER VINEYARDS

GRAPE CREEK VINEYARDS

SISTER CREEK VINEYARDS

Stonewall

BELL MOUNTAIN VINEYARDS

16

Fredericksburg

1376

Luckenbach

Sisterdale

FREDERICKSBURG WINERY

THE ENCHANTED TRAIL WINERIES

❧Becker Vineyards

P.O. Box 813, Stonewall, Texas 78671

Phone: (830) 644-2681, Fax: (830) 644-2773

OPEN: 10 A.M.–5 P.M.
MONDAY–SATURDAY;
12–5 P.M. SUNDAY

TASTINGS, RETAIL SALES, AND
GIFTS, BED AND BREAKFAST

BECKER VINEYARDS

TEXAS
1996
FUME BLANC
CELLARED AND BOTTLED BY BECKER VINEYARDS,
FREDERICKSBURG, TX BW-TX-91 ALCOHOL 12.5% BY VOLUME CONTAINS SULFITES

Richard and Bunny Becker planted their experimental thirteen-acre vineyard in the overgrown remnants of a peanut farm surrounded by an ancient stand of mustang grapes. As the Beckers' excitement grew, they quickly expanded the young vineyard to thirty-six acres of French vinifera grapes in 1993 and began restoration work on the original German farmhouse. The Beckers developed their site to resemble an early nineteenth-century country farm, complete with windmill, log cabin and barn. The cabin has been remodeled to serve as a bed and breakfast at the winery.

Visitors approach the winery (which was built to resemble a Hill Country German stone barn) through a field of grapevines

GERMAN INFLUENCE IS EVIDENT IN THE DESIGN OF BECKER
VINEYARDS WINERY.

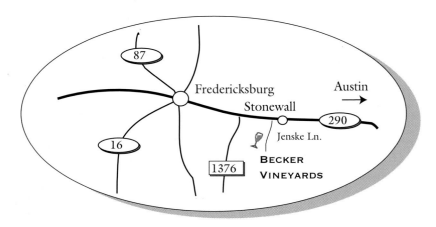

BECKER VINEYARDS

with yellow rose bushes planted at the end of each row. From the front porch, the view extends across a wildflower field to a vineyard of Sauvignon Blanc. From the back porch the view extends across a field of bluebonnets to a twenty-five-acre vineyard. The Beckers have expanded the original thirteen-acre test vineyard to a thirty-six-acre vineyard at the time of this writing. Richard Becker planted classic French grapes: Chardonnay, Cabernet Sauvignon, Cabernet Franc, Malbec, Petit Verdot, and Merlot, along with an unusual group of Rhone varietals: Viognier, Syrah, Mourvedre, Greneche, Roussanne, and Marsanne. The Viognier vineyard is the first significant effort of its kind in Texas.

The Beckers have dedicated acreage not planted with vineyards to raising Texas wildflowers for seed harvesting. As a result, each spring their winery has the distinction of being surrounded by vast expanses of some of the most beautiful Texas wildflowers including bluebonnets, cosmos, and Indian paintbrush.

THE WINES

This is truly a winery with a wonderful future. The Beckers opened the doors of their tasting room in June 1996, offering only a limited selection of white wines, a Muscat Canelli and a Sauvignon Blanc, while a full compliment of red wines aged in French oak barrels in the wine cellar.

Since 1996, Becker Vineyards has been offering Chardonnay, Sauvignon Blanc, Semillion, Cabernet Sauvignon, Cabernet Franc, Merlot, Malbec, and Petit Verdot. They also produce the rare Viognier—a wine originally made in France during the days of the Roman Empire.

Becker Vineyards produce their Fume Blanc in the classic style of a white Bordeaux, using eighty percent Sauvignon Blanc and twenty percent Semillion grapes. Their Chardonnay undergoes primary and secondary **malolactic** fermentation with aging surlies in French oak, resulting in the familiar buttery, rich flavor. Red wines are produced with primary and secondary fermentation in stainless-steel tanks followed by aging in French oak barrels.

A MAGNIFICENT TASTING ROOM
AWAITS VISITORS.

ROWS OF
GLYCOL-JACKETED
STAINLESS STEEL
FERMENTATION TANKS.

WINE BARRELS ARE OFTEN STACKED
TO INCREASE A BARREL ROOM'S
STORAGE CAPACITY.

Becker Vineyards celebrated its first anniversary on the Fourth of July 1997 with a grand party. There was music, food, wine, and even a cannon shoot! Mr. Becker's purchase of a cannon was a surprise to everyone. As his daughter, and integral part of the wine team, explained, "Dad just came home with a cannon one day, and we all thought, now what!" Of course, Mr. Becker knew exactly what he was doing; the cannon shoot has proved to be a very popular feature of the winery.

DIRECTIONS: FROM BECKER VINEYARDS, IT IS A SHORT TRIP WEST ON SH 290 UNTIL YOU SEE THE SIGN FOR GRAPE CREEK VINEYARDS ON YOUR LEFT.

♣Grape Creek Vineyards

SH 290, Stonewall, Texas
Phone: (830) 644-2710, Fax: (830) 644-2746

OPEN: 10 A.M.–5 P.M.
MONDAY–SATURDAY;
12–5 P.M. SUNDAY

TASTINGS, RETAIL SALES,
AND GIFTS

Grape Creek
VINEYARD
1996
TEXAS
CABERNET ROUGE
83.3% Cabernet Sauvignon, 16.7% Syrah
Semi-Sweet
Produced & Bottled by Grape Creek Vineyard, Inc.
Stonewall, Gillespie County, Texas
Alcohol By Volume 11.0%   750 ML

Anyone who has driven on SH 290 from Houston to Fredericksburg will no doubt recognize the name Grape Creek Vineyards. This vineyard, planted by owner Ned Simes in 1985, is perhaps one of the most visible and accessible wineries in the Hill Country. The winery's popularity was underscored for us during a visit on a July 4th weekend when the holiday rush of visitors was taken in stride by the owners and staff. The gracious hospitality extended in the tasting room and the well-versed tour guide makes a visit to Grape Creek enjoyable any time of the year.

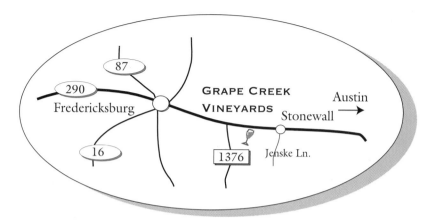

GRAPE CREEK VINEYARDS

Grape Creek is a self-described "boutique winery," a term that may confuse many consumers who associate the word boutique with specialty retail stores. In the context of this industry, a boutique winery is one that specializes in a small number of high-quality wines offered in limited bottling. The efforts of the Simes family fit this definition quite well.

In addition to the fine selection of wines, the Simeses offer possibly the most impressive selections of trinkets available in all the Hill Country wineries. In their tasting room, a visitor may choose from an assortment of wine accessories, toys made from corks, flavored vinegars, and even wine-scented soap.

THE ENTRY TO GRAPE CREEK VINEYARDS ON SH 290.

**THE MAGNIFICENT STONEWORK OF EARLY GERMAN SETTLERS IS
ECHOED IN THE GRAPE CREEK'S MAIN BUILDING.**

As part of the tour, visitors are led down to the wine cellar to view future wines as they age in oak barrels. Grape Creek has one of the few active, fully functional wine cellars in Texas. It is a particular favorite with visitors because it has an atmosphere most people associate with a winery. Wineries and wine cellars go hand-in-hand in the minds of many, and Grape Creek is uniquely able to provide that imagery.

Ned Simes purchased the property, nestled alongside Grape Creek in Stonewall, following a long search across the United States. After submitting soil samples to A&M University for testing to verify his selection, Ned knew that the climate and soil conditions in this area of the Hill Country were perfect for producing quality grapes. He submitted additional soil samples in 1994 and projected plans to expand the vineyard in ten-acre plots for the next three to four years.

As is the case with many other smaller wineries in Texas, the owner is also the winemaker, vine pruner, harvester, bottler, and sales representative. On any given weekend, you will find Ned and his family in the tasting room giving tours and explaining the different wines being tasted. On any given weekday, you will find Ned and his son Lee in the vineyard tending to the fruit, or in the winery, nurturing the next vintage.

The Simeses deeply believe in the value of family heritage and what it means to producing wines. Ned's son Lee, who shares the responsibility of the vineyard and the winery with his father, was quick to explain the family's commitment to producing fine quality wines. Lee's wife, described by many as having one of the best "noses" in the business, is a major influence in the blending of the wines here.

THE WINES

Grape Creek produces six wines, all made in the French style of winemaking: Cabernet Sauvignon, Cabernet Trois, Cabernet Blanc, Chardonnay, Fumé Blanc, and Sauvignon Blanc. More recently, the Simeses have experimented with a Christmas wine called Holiday Rouge, a Cabernet Sauvignon fermented on the skins, pressed not too harshly, and then allowed to achieve a three-percent residual sugar content. The result is a cherry-colored, very drinkable semi-sweet wine to be enjoyed during the holiday season.

The Simeses only produce their Cabernet Sauvignons when the crop quality meets their high standards, which explains why the wine was produced in 1989 and 1990 but not in the following two years. Their 1993 Cabernet Sauvignon in still is oak and is expected to age for another six months before bottling. A 1989 vintage opened during the 1994 holiday season displayed a well-balanced taste and deep crimson color, having matured beautifully in the bottle.

Grape Creek's Fumé Blanc is normally one hundred percent Sauvignon Blanc. In 1994, however, the Simes experimented by blending in a small percentage of Semillion grapes before introducing the wine into French oak. The experimental twist to their winemaking philosophy is a refreshing addition to the Texas wine industry. One of their experiments in 1993, the Cabernet Trois, has turned out to be a huge success. A blend of Cabernet Sauvignon, Cabernet Franc, and Ruby Cabernet, this wine is ideal for the consumer who enjoys a red wine, but does not like the heavier taste of a Merlot or Cabernet Sauvignon.

DIRECTIONS: FROM GRAPE CREEK VINEYARDS WE TRAVEL WEST ON SH 290 FOR APPROXIMATELY 19 MILES TO THE TOWN OF FREDERICKSBURG, TURNING NORTH ON SH 16. BELL MOUNTAIN VINEYARDS IS 14 MILES NORTH OF TOWN.

❧Bell Mountain Vineyards

HC 61, Box 22, Fredericksburg, Texas 78624
Phone: (830) 685-3297, Fax: (830) 685-3657

OPEN: 12–5 P.M.
SATURDAYS ONLY

TASTINGS, RETAIL SALES,
AND GIFTS

BELL MOUNTAIN
ESTATE BOTTLED

Cabernet Sauvignon

1995 bell mountain

12% ALCOHOL BY VOLUME
Grown, Produced & Bottled by
BELL MOUNTAIN VINEYARDS
Fredericksburg, Texas

Located north of Fredericksburg on the slopes of Bell Mountain is Bell Mountain/Oberhellman Vineyards. Originally known as Oberhellman Vineyards, owner/winemaker Robert (Bob) Oberhellman changed the winery's name to honor the areas designation in 1986 as Texas' first appellation area. This identifies the area as possessing unique soil and climatic characteristics for producing quality grapes for winemaking.

Spreading across the rolling foothills of Bell Mountain, the winery's vineyards have slowly grown from thirty acres in 1986 to fifty-five acres in 1993. According to his wife Evelyn, this methodical expansion of the vineyard is indicative of Bob's ap-

THE WINERY'S ARCHITECTURE MIMICS BUILDINGS FOUND IN
GERMANY'S COUNTRYSIDE.

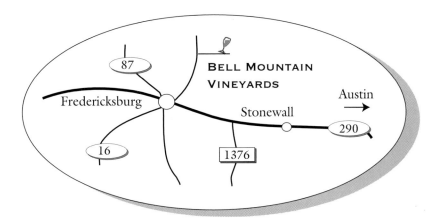

BELL MOUNTAIN VINEYARDS

proach to every aspect of the winery. "The facilities have grown in a similar fashion," Evelyn tells us, "following Bob's master plan." Using a phased approach to expand the facility, the Oberhellmans have incorporated a spacious brick patio to separate the original lab/office building from the winery itself and have purchased state-of-the-art winemaking equipment. The patio, equipped with a large masonry barbecue and wine-barrel tables, is enjoyed by visitors to the winery and local organizations who hold charitable functions in this beautiful setting.

Bob Oberhellman's approach to wine has been influenced by the winemaking education he received in France and California, as well as his work experience in the food industry. It is not surprising that Bob views wine as a food product and considers his estate-bottled wines as fine dinner wines. His food-industry experience provides Bell Mountain Vineyards with another critical business element for a growing winery: marketing expertise. Bell Mountain wines enjoy wide distribution throughout Texas and are easily obtained at major liquor stores.

THE WINES

The careful balancing of European and Californian techniques has been a pivotal factor in the production of Bell Mountain premium wines. Along with the traditional techniques of the European masters that emphasize the "art" of winemaking, Bob uses the latest research and technology from California that have revolutionized modern winemaking.

Planted primarily with Old-World grapes, Bob's vineyard grows Chardonnay, Johannisberg Riesling, Gewurztraminer, Sauvignon Blanc, Semillion, Cabernet Sauvignon, Merlot, and Pinot Noir. Locate at an elevation of 2,000 feet, the vineyards are planted at 725 plants per acre and use a six-foot-high trellis for maximum foliage development. These techniques allow Bob to produce approximately 3,200 cases each year.

The white wines are prepared in the traditional German method. After crushing and destemming, the white grapes are pressed immediately. Once separated from the skins, the juice is rapidly chilled and cultured yeast is introduced prior to refrigeration in stainless-steel vats at 50–55°F. These low temperatures allow for very slow fermentation that preserves the delicate fruit of the grape. After bottling, the wines continue to age for two to six months. Bob requires that all of Bell Mountain white wines remain in the bottle for at least a year prior to being release for sale.

The Riesling has all the classic characteristics you would expect from German wine—blossomy, rich grapefruit and apricot flavors finished to a medium-sweet flavor by subtle acidity. When asked to speak about this wine, Bob claims, "It is the only true Riesling made in Texas."

Bell Mountain red wines are fermented on their skins for seven days to extract the desired color and flavor. After pressing, they are then placed in French oak, American oak, or stainless-steel tanks for aging and **fined** with egg whites prior to bottling. After bottling, the reds continue to age for six to twelve months. Bell Mountain red wines must be in the bottle for well over a year before being released.

The Oberhellmans offer a variety of wines under a second label, Oberhoff Vineyards. These tend to be fruitier, sweeter wines, with somewhat whimsical names such as the Christmas favorite Kristkindl, a mead-type wine best served warm, and Blushin' Bertha, a fun, informal blush wine.

For Bob and Evelyn, the winery's location has had some surprising benefits. It is not an exaggeration to say that the winery is off the beaten path compared to other wineries in the area; you have to intentionally be going to this winery. Visitors are typically wine lovers who have heard about these wines from friends or from conversations with folks in Fredericksburg. The residents of the town are proud of the local wineries and are generous with directions.

DIRECTIONS: WE STOP OUR TOUR HERE FOR TODAY TO ENJOY THE DOWNTOWN AREA OF FREDERICKSBURG. TOMORROW, AFTER ENJOYING AN OLD-FASHIONED BREAKFAST AT A BED AND BREAKFAST OR AT ONE OF THE LOCAL RESTAURANTS AND BAKERIES, WE WILL VISIT THE FREDERICKSBURG WINERY BEFORE LEAVING FOR THE TOWN OF SISTERDALE.

Fredericksburg Winery

247 West Main, Fredericksburg, Texas 78624

Phone: (830) 990-8747, Fax: (830) 990-8566

OPEN: 10 A.M.–6 P.M.
MONDAY–THURSDAY
10 A.M.–6 P.M.
FRIDAY–SATURDAY; 11 A.M.–6
P.M. SUNDAY

TASTINGS, RETAIL SALES,
AND GIFTS

Fredericksburg, Texas
Baron's Bach Burgundy
Texas Cabernet Sauvignon
1993

The road to the Fredericksburg Winery has been a long one for the Switzer family. Along the way there have been long hours, dedication, setbacks, and success. But it has mostly been a story of what a family can do when they believe in each other. Opening in 1995 on Main Street in downtown Fredericksburg, this winery is a showplace for all Texas wines, Texas food products, and a large selection of wine accessories.

The family has put their heart and soul into producing a marvelous selection of wines. Stop by the winery on any weekend and three generations will be behind the counter. On our last visit, the Switzer brothers, their seventy-seven-year-old mother,

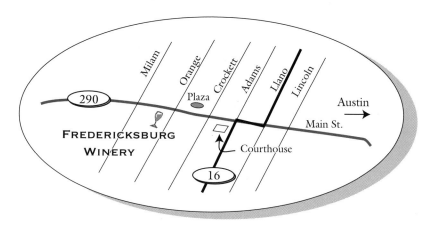

FREDERICKSBURG WINERY

both their wives, and Jene's five-year-old daughter, Chardonnay, were all helping.

Jene Switzer, winemaker extraordinaire, may possibly be the hardest working winemaker in the Texas wine industry. Prior to opening the family winery, Jene served five wineries in Texas in positions ranging from vineyard manager to winemaker. Over the past twenty years, he has consistently produced some of the best wines in Texas.

We first met Jene in the summer of 1993 at the Hill Country Cellars in Cedar Park, Texas. There he was assisting Russell Smith (winemaker at that time) with a recent harvest. At that time, Jene was also working with the Wimberley Valley Winery, producing a small bottling of his own under the name of Falcon Hills Cellars.

Shortly after that, Jene and his brother Cord established The Great Texas Champagne Winery Company in Johnson City to produce and market the Falcon Hills label. The wines were primarily late harvest, which means the grapes had been allowed to ripen on the vine longer, which increases the sugar content of the grape and develops a sweeter wine. This style of wine—unique in Texas—has earned many awards for the Switzer family.

After a year of operating from the Johnson City location, Jene and Cord decided to join the exciting atmosphere being created by the wineries in the Fredericksburg area. The Fredericksburg Winery is the culmination of years of patience and hard work. The winery offers twenty-three wines for tasting seven days a week. With a current capacity of approximately 5,000 cases, Jene releases a remarkable array of wines ranging from standard varietals to his famous late-harvest wines. During our October '97 visit, six new wines were released, and three more were due by the end of the year.

THE WINES

The Switzers acquired the Bakersfield Experimental Vineyard from the University of Texas in 1998. Jene has been modifying his winemaking technique recently, and has decided to use ex-

A WINE'S CHARACTER IS A COMBINATION OF THE GRAPE, THE VINEYARD, AND THE WINEMAKER'S SKILL.
(COURTESY OF THE TEXAS DEPARTMENT OF AGRICULTURE)

tended skin contact for all of his wines to deepen the color and character of the juice. How he manages to produce such a large selection of wines from an extremely compact facility is a mystery. He only admits that work often goes on long into the night after the winery closes its doors.

As the variety of the wines increases, so does the number of awards the winery receives. Their "Newsom" Orange Muscat Late Harvest Vinter's Select Reserve won a silver medal and the Scheurebe, Late Harvest Special Reserve won a bronze medal at the 1997 World Wine Championships. Jene expected their Erstfliegen Sherry 1996 Palamino—the first Sherry released by a Texas winery—to do well in the 1998 competition.

One of the most exciting things about the Switzer family is their zest for experimenting. They have broken with tradition by giving most of their wines German names, such as Versuchs Weinberg Late Harvest Scheurebe, Freiwilliger Johannisberg Riesling and Zelebration (a white table wine). Each wine's name refers to a Texas story or tradition that is explained on the back of the bottle.

The bottles used by the winery are also part of their experimentation, from the tall square bottle of the Newsom Orange Muscate to the beautifully etched, wide-bodied style for the Sherry. Many of these bottles are likely to become collector's items.

The Switzer family's love for wine shows in all aspects of their work, from the wine itself, to the congenial reception each visitor is given on stepping into their tasting room. Be sure to talk a while with Cord and Jene—their knowledge of winemaking, grape growing, and the Texas wine industry is vast.

DIRECTIONS: LEAVING FREDERICKSBURG, WE HEAD EAST ON SH 290 TO ROUTE 1346 AND TURN SOUTH, FOR OUR LAST STOP ON THE ENCHANTED TRAIL, SISTER CREEK VINEYARDS IN THE HISTORIC TOWN OF SISTERDALE. ROUTE 1346 OFFERS ROLLING HILLS, JUTTING HILL TOPS, AND ORNATE RANCH ENTRANCE GATES.

ABOUT 15 MILES SOUTH OF SH 290 IS THE FIVE-RESIDENT TOWN OF LUCKENBACH, EULOGIZED BY COUNTRY AND WESTERN SINGERS. STOP IN TO HAVE A COLD BEER OR SODA WITH WHOEVER HAPPENS TO BE SITTING UNDER THE TREES NEXT TO THE GENERAL STORE.

❧Sister Creek Vineyards

1142 Sisterdale, Sisterdale, Texas

Phone: (830) 324-6704, Fax: (830) 324-6704

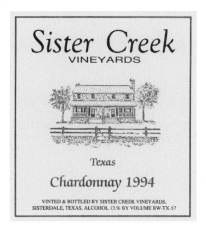

Heading south on Route 1346, we begin the eighteen-mile drive through the Great Divide—the High Hills that separate the Pedernales River watershed from the Guadalupe River watershed. This sparsely populated area offers breathtaking scenery on our drive to the town of Sisterdale. If you own a convertible, this is the perfect road to drive.

Sister Creek Vineyards is hard to miss in this town of 25 people. The winery is housed in a renovated 100-year-old cotton gin, the largest structure in Sisterdale. The vineyard, consisting of three acres of lush vines planted along the town's Main Street, dominates the landscape.

Owner Vernon Fiesenham and winemaker Danny Hernandez started the vineyard in the 1986–87 season, in a valley of rich alluvial soil between west and east Sister Creeks. They originally planted the vineyard at an 8 × 12 density (8 feet between vines and 12 feet between rows); the next year they planted in between the existing vines to double the density. At this double density, Vernon and Danny began using an open canopy type of wiring trellis throughout the vineyard. "The open canopy requires more labor," says Danny, "but it opens the vines to more sunlight."

THE WINES

During the first three years of vineyard production, Danny had to bring in grapes from the Lubbock area to supplement the young

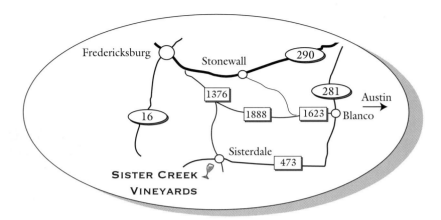

Fredericksburg

Stonewall

290

1376

281

Austin

16

1888

1623

Blanco

Sisterdale

473

SISTER CREEK
VINEYARDS

SISTER CREEK VINEYARDS

harvests. Today, with 3,000 vines on three acres, the winery's vineyard produces enough Cabernet Sauvignon, Pinot Noir, Merlot, and Cabernet Franc to allow Sister Creek's first estate bottling in 1994. The fruit harvested from these three acres is sufficient for their annual production, which never exceeds 800 gallons.

Sister Creek produces two subtle, elegant wines, a Chardonnay and a Cabernet Sauvignon. The small size of the winery allows Danny to carefully control the winemaking process (from vineyard to barrel) and test experimental techniques. He prefers not to filter his wines when possible to maintain as much flavor and character of the grape as possible.

Sister Creek's Chardonnay is a diamond-in-the-rough, a consistently remarkable wine from this tiny hamlet winery in the Hill Country. Danny leaves the fruit in contact with the skins for twelve hours to enhance the fruit flavor with eighty percent malolactic fermentation to soften the acidity and introduce that "buttery" flavor. It is then fermented in stainless steel with 100 percent lees (sediment) contact for one to two months, then aged in French oak. The result is a wine with a subtle oak "nose" and a hint of cinnamon to round out the taste.

The Cabernet Sauvignon is a classic production, fruity and clean with a crisp structure and deep ruby color. "The best reception for these Cabs" explains Danny, "has been when they are blended with thirty percent Cabernet Franc." Sister Creek Cabernet Sauvignon is aged for two years in French oak with no filtering.

When asked about future plans for the winery, Danny echoes Vernon's desire to keep the winery small for the foreseeable future. "We currently sell all that we produce," explains Danny, "and have no plans to market our wines beyond the Fredericksburg area in the near future." Sister Creek wines may be purchased at the winery's tasting room, and from the two independent tasting rooms in downtown Fredericksburg.

Sister Creek Vineyards is our last winery along the Enchanted Trail. For those who enjoy antique shopping or just want to stop for lunch before heading home, travel south on 1346 to the town of Boerne. Another old German town, Boerne is reminiscent of Fredericksburg with its selection of shops, restaurants, and historic downtown district.

ALONG THE TRAIL

The Enchanted Trail best captures the flavor of the Hill Country's German heritage. Remnants of that past are preserved in towns such as Boerne, Comfort, and best of all, along our wine trail in towns like Fredericksburg and Sisterdale. The Enchanted Trail is a superb combination of the natural beauty that typifies the Hill Country and the excitement of towns rich in the culture, food, art, and the heritage of the Old World. Towns like Fredericksburg fill visitors with a peacefulness born partly of the slower lifestyle there, and partly with their romantic, settled qualities.

Fredericksburg is an enigma, representing different things to different people. For some, it is a wondrous collection of antique shops, for others a charismatic German town, and for yet others, a romantic getaway. In reality, it is all of these and more. The town fathers painstakingly preserved the original architecture of the German immigrants, who were masters in carpentry and masonry. Renovations to storefronts along Main Street preserve original designs; Sunday Homes and log cabins have been converted to bed and breakfasts, and the original extra-wide streets (for turning teams of horses) remain.

The rich assortment of bed and breakfasts and the people they attract help to explain another facet of the atmosphere that fills the town—romance. You can spot it everywhere, couples walking hand-in-hand along Main Street, kissing at intersections and snuggling close in the beer gardens of German restaurants.

Enchanted Rock State Park lies just to the north of Fredericksburg. Visitors have two routes to reach Enchanted Rock from Fredericksburg: by turning north off Main Street and proceeding 18 miles on Milam Street, which becomes FM 965. The second route is to drive north on SH 16 for 21 miles, then turn west onto FM 965 for another 8 miles to the park. Enchanted Rock is the second largest outcropping of pink granite in the United States after Georgia's Stone Mountain. Entrance to the park costs $5, and you can expect crowds during the summer months.

In the springtime, wine tourists are treated to splendid displays of the Texas bluebonnets and Indian paintbrush flowers that carpet the medians and sides of SH 290 between Austin and Fredericksburg. In June, the treat is peaches. The peach harvest is dominant this time of year, with peach stands lining the roads near the Stonewall and Fredericksburg areas.

The harshness and drama of pioneer life in the Hill Country becomes obvious if you tour the city cemetery in Fredericksburg. The German settlers brought their beliefs and traditions with them, as evidenced in the ornate ironworks that box in burial sites. Indications of the devastating epidemics that ravaged pioneer life can be seen in the number of tiny graves of pioneer children who fell victim to these diseases.

HIGHLAND TRAIL WINERIES

The winding roads of the Highland Trail offers you dramatic views of the seven Highland Lakes. These azure blue lakes come into view momentarily, briefly disappear, then burst into view along the next turn. This trail offers a pleasant day-long ride through the hills and valleys that are home to these seven man-made lakes. There are six wineries in this northern section of the Hill Country: Hill Country Cellars, Fall Creek Vineyards, Spicewood Vineyards, Slaughter-Leftwich, Cana Cellars Winery, and Oak Hill Cellars. At this writing, Spicewood Vineyards requires an appointment and Oak Hill Cellars is not open to the public.

With only four of the Highland Trail wineries opened to the public, this may seem like a quick trip to many of you not familiar with the area. Take heed however, the trail's length can be deceiving. As an example, the journey through the magnificent countryside between Hill Country Cellars and Fall Creek Vineyards is around two hours. Since most of these wineries close at 5:00 P.M., be sure to arrive at Hill Country Cellars around opening time. Then enjoy an early afternoon drive along Route 1431 to Fall Creek Vineyards, then work your way back down to the Austin area wineries.

First stop is the metropolitan-like environment surrounding Hill Country Cellars in Cedar Park just north of Austin. After enjoying these aromatic wines, we travel along the winding lakeside roads to one of the oldest wineries, Fall Creek Vineyards. Fall Creek Vineyards, located at the northern tip of Lake Buchanan, is the place where the Auler's have been making outstanding wines for over a decade. Next, (if you have made an appointment) we head back toward Austin to visit one of the newest Texas wineries, Spicewood Vineyards, in the town of Spicewood. Continuing along SH 71, we visit another Highland Lakes treasure—the French-styled hillside winery Slaughter-Leftwich Vineyards overlooking Lake Travis. If the wines and views from the patio of Slaughter-Leftwich haven't left you too light headed, we continue to our last stop on the trail, Cana Cellars Winery.

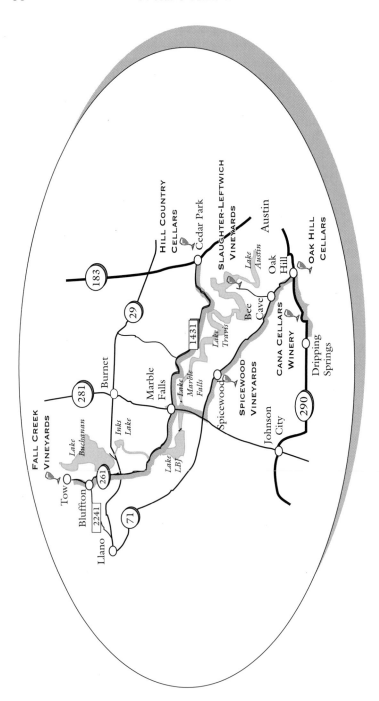

♣Hill Country Cellars

1700 North Bell Blvd., Cedar Park, Texas 78613
Phone: (512) 259-200, (800) 264-7273, Fax: (512) 259-2092

TOURS: 1–4 P.M. FRIDAY–SUNDAY
ON THE HOUR

TASTINGS: 12–5 P.M. DAILY

RETAIL SALES AND GIFT SHOP

FREDERICK THOMAS
1995

TEXAS
MERLOT

ALCOHOL 13.2% BY VOLUME

HILL COUNTRY CELLARS

The rural backdrop of the Hill Country Cellars compound, juxtaposed against the hustle and bustle of SH 183, offers a unique setting for a winery. Those travelers who manage to spot the small sign that marks the entrance to the winery are in for a real treat.

Through thoughtful planning, developer Fred Thomas has managed to create an environment reminiscent of a small French country winery. The original farmhouse has been transformed into a charming tasting room, which also serves as a passageway into the modern production facility. Visitors to Hill Country Cellars are encouraged to stroll among the huge live oaks surrounding the facilities or enjoy the cool, shaded deck that overlooks the vineyard.

While enjoying the gracefully landscaped gardens, be sure to visit the 200-year-old mustang grapevine that Fred saved from the wrecking ball. This gnarled, fruit-bearing vine was transplanted—along with the oak tree it is attached to—from the site of the old schoolhouse in Cedar Park. Hill Country Cellars is working toward obtaining a historical classification for the vine.

Winemaker Anne Smith walked us through the four acres of vine that recently fell victim to Pierce's disease. As a result, the majority of the grapes used in their wines come from West Texas. Like many wineries in Texas, Hill Country Cellars draws from a wide selection of vineyard sites across Texas as a hedge against inclement weather. At this writing, the decision to replant the

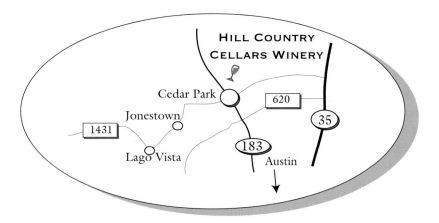

HILL COUNTRY CELLARS WINERY

THE VINEYARDS AROUND HILL COUNTRY CELLARS.

vineyard had not been made. If replanting is decided on, Anne tells us that she will prefer the hardy black Spanish grape, Lenoir, which is resistant to Pierce's disease.

Anne's winemaking philosophy is similar to other winemakers who possess a true love of the craft and combine the vision and skill of the purist with the common sense of the realist. She tries to let the wines express themselves, striving for consistency yet complexity, while allowing the wines to be drinkable immediately.

THE WINES

Judging by recent product offerings, the developer and the winemaker have much to be proud of in their award-winning wines. The Hill Country Cellars Chardonnay is consistently one of the best available from the Hill Country wineries. All of the wines made here share a marvelous characteristic: each possesses a wonderful "nose," whether it's the Chardonnay or the Hill Country Blush table wine.

Hill Country Cellars red wines include Cabernet Sauvignon, Merlot, Ranch Red, Ruby Cabernet, and a Port, called Don Thomas, named after the owner's father. In addition to their Chardonnay, other white wines include a Sauvignon Blanc, Chenin Blanc, Johannisberg Riesling, and Texas Star Spumante—a champagne-style wine, once made by a former Texas winery that Mr. Thomas purchased the rights from to continue producing the sparkling wine.

Anne is especially proud of the winery's Chardonnay, which she produces in a fashion similar to the methods used by previous winemakers at Hill Country Cellars. To add her own touch, however, Anne blends French and American oak fermentation into her Chardonnay—something she feels adds a superior quality to the final taste of the wine. Somewhat of a forward thinker, Anne was one of the first in the state to offer a wine made from "American" grapes rather than "Texas" grapes. The shortage of Texas grapes over the past few years has had most vintners struggling to find enough grapes to produce consistent volumes of wine. Anne was the lone wolf when she started, but now a number of Texas wineries offer wines made from "American" grapes as well as "Texas" grapes.

Future plans for their wines were still up in the air when we spoke in late 1997. The scarcity of red grapes was complicating the winery's long-range plans. As Anne told us, "We won't know what we'll be doing until the first quarter of next year, depending on what grapes are available."

An active calendar of events throughout the year, including a grape stomping and the Octoberfest celebration, makes this winery an exciting place to visit. The owners are making plans to enhance the facilities and expand the events roster.

DIRECTIONS: AFTER ENJOYING OUR WINE TASTING AND A REST UNDER THE MAGNIFICENT OAK TREES THAT SHADE THE SPACIOUS DECK SURROUNDING HILL COUNTRY CELLARS TASTING ROOM, WE TRAVEL WEST ON ROUTE 1431 TO VISIT FALL CREEK VINEYARDS. KEEP THOSE CAMERAS READY! THIS TWISTING, TURNING ROAD, WHICH HUGS THE HILLSIDES ALONG THE HIGHLAND LAKES, OFFERS SOME INCREDIBLE VIEWS.

❧Fall Creek Vineyards

Located 2.2 miles north of the post office
Tow, Texas
Mailing address: 1111 Guadalupe St., Austin, Tx 78701
Phone: (512) 476-4477 or (915) 379-5361

> OPEN: 11 A.M.–3 P.M.
> MONDAY–FRIDAY; 12–5 P.M.
> SATURDAY; 12–4 P.M. SUNDAYS
> (MARCH–NOVEMBER)
>
> TOURS, TASTINGS, RETAIL SALES,
> AND GIFT SHOP

If you have never visited the Lake Buchanan area, you will find that this part of the Hill Country boasts some of the most beautiful landscape in Texas. Traveling these winding roads, you will be hard-pressed to run out of unique and beautiful locations to experience. It is in this dramatic setting that we find ourselves, on our way to Fall Creek Vineyards.

Fall Creek Vineyards produces quality wines on sixty-five acres along the sandy loam shore of Lake Buchanan. This entire area rests on a large plateau that provides a special climate for growing grapes in Texas. The breeze coming from the lake creates an evening cooling effect perfect for vineyard conditions.

Ed and Susan Auler, the owners of Fall Creek Vineyards, have contributed much time and energy to their own endeavor as well as the Texas wine industry. Ed uses his legal background to help develop legislation for the Texas wine industry, while Susan uses her excellent organizational skills to help produce wine events around the state. One event held in early April, The Texas Hill Country Wine and Food Festival, brings together seminars, wine tasting, and an all-day festival of Texas wine and food producers. This event is an enjoyable blending of Texas wines, foods, and music. A weekend of sampling the wines and foods of Texas offers information and culinary treats found only in the Austin area.

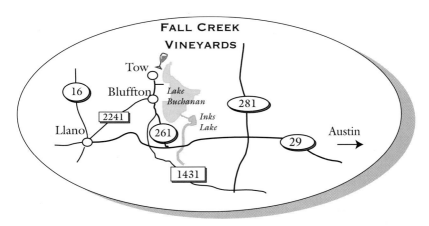

FALL CREEK VINEYARDS

Ed Auler's original experimentation with grafting in 1980 proved to be rewarding. By grafting onto champanel rootstock, he brought together the quality of his performing vinifera with the disease resistance of the rootstock to produce a superb grape capable of withstanding attack from diseases such as phylloxera and nematodes. This proved to Ed that vineyards in Texas could grow the best known selections of wine-producing grapes. In 1990, preferable rootstocks were introduced to Fall Creek, and since then the entire vineyard has been regrafted to improve the quality and production.

Along with the vintners of northeast Texas, the Aulers work to enact favorable wine legislation and have made a great contribution to the wine industry in Texas. It became evident to these visionaries that the best wine area of Texas just happened to be located in dry counties and legislation would be needed to change the law in these areas for growth and development of the industry. The production and sale of wine is against the law in these areas. Some dry counties have adopted their laws to allow the growing of grapes, but not the consumption of the alcohol product. These same visionaries are still active today in the legislative process to help make the changes needed to produce and market their wine products in these select areas of Texas.

THE WINES

The Fall Creek Vineyards site on the Colorado River has a history as old as Texas. The Indians that lived on this land left behind a variety of artifacts along their burial mounds and in the Fall Creek Vineyard fields. The burial mounds have been left undisturbed, but arrowheads are often found after heavy rains and are on display in the Fall Creek tasting room. This land was understandably in demand even back then. The property contains innumerable microclimates and rich soils, perfect for grape maturation. After the Aulers spent more than a decade of growing premium grapes at Fall Creek Vineyards, however, a severe frost in 1991 destroyed most of their premier vines. Inspired by the adversity, the Aulers shifted focus, found other sources in Texas for grapes, and continued to produce premium wines while they replanted their vineyard in stages.

Today Fall Creek Vineyards award-winning wines are in such great demand that its sells all it produces. Their Chardonnay enhances the grape's character through cold fermentation and about thirty percent oak aging for four months. A great Chardonnay substitute is their Vintner's Cuvee, which is a blend of Chardonnay and Chenin Blanc, fermented in oak and having undergone partial malolactic fermentation. Just prior to bottling, a small amount of Muscat Canelli is added, giving the wine a slightly fruitier taste.

The Fall Creek Vineyards red wines undergo oak aging in a combination of American and French oak. The Merlot is a blend of Merlot, Malbec and Cabernet Franc, resulting in a fruity, medium-bodied wine. The Cabernet Sauvignon—which has a habit of selling out very quickly is a wine with soft tannins that allow for immediate consumption, but it is also able to age for years to come.

Additional wine favorites include Cascade, White Zinfandel, and the "Granite" wines: Granite Reserve and Granite Blush. The Granite wine series has been particularly popular with consumers and usually quickly disappear. The Granite Reserve is a blend of Cabernet Sauvignon, Merlot, and Malbec, which produces a soft wine that is ready to be consumed with less bottle aging. The Granite Blush is a blend of Johannisberg Riesling, Chenin Blanc, and Cabernet Sauvignon and is slightly drier than most blush wines.

Since its inception, Fall Creek has made a commitment to quality wines by harmonizing the best European winemaking techniques with the best technological innovations of this century. Its success is underscored by the demand for its wines, which greatly exceeds the supply.

Fall Creek also maintains an active schedule of events during the year. The most popular by far is the Grape Stomp Celebration held every August on the last two Saturdays prior to Labor Day weekend. The event features food, music, lake cruises, and fun activities for the kids.

ACTIVITIES IN THE AREA

If you enjoy outdoor activities, you may want to linger in this area after your visit to Fall Creek Vineyards. There are a variety of state parks and recreational areas around Lake Buchanan and Inks Lake offering camping and water sports. The Inks Lake State Park is a beautiful area that draws many artists to reflect and paint. Golf, swimming, boating, and fishing provide entertainment to please the whole family. A small admission fee is charged for the state park. One of the highlighted attractions in this area is the Vanishing Texas River Cruise. Tours along the banks of Lake Buchanan offer some of the best picturesque scenery in the Hill Country. Tours are two and a half or four hours long. Special cruises running from November through February feature a close look at the American bald eagle that migrates to this area.

DIRECTIONS: WE LEAVE THE BUCOLIC SETTING ALONG LAKE BUCHANAN TO CONTINUE OUR TRAIL WITH A VISIT TO SPICEWOOD VINEYARDS. WE WILL TAKE FM 2241 TO SH 261, AND TURN EAST ON SH 29, THEN HEAD SOUTH ON IH 281. ONE AREA ESPECIALLY WORTH NOTING ALONG SH 29 IS THE INTERLAKE AREA BETWEEN LAKE BUCHANAN AND INKS LAKE.

❧Spicewood Vineyards

P.O. Box 248, Spicewood, Texas 78669
Phone: (210) 693-5328, Fax: (210) 693-5940

THE WINERY IS NOT OPEN TO THE PUBLIC. TOURS AND TASTINGS MAY BE ARRANGED BY APPOINTMENT.

NO RETAIL SALES ARE AVAILABLE.

Now this is Texas! Located thirty-five miles north of Austin, Spicewood Vineyards is a bit of a challenge to find. Heading south along SH 71, if you pass the Exxon station at the intersection of SH 71 and SH 191, well pardner, you've gone too far! At this writing there was no "Winery" sign to mark the turn onto Route 408, a small two-lane highway. Your only landmark is Cypress Creek, which flows under SH 71. Once on Route 408, you follow a twisting road for a mile or two to Route 409. The "Manigold" sign nailed to an oak tree tells you where Route 409 is before the highway sign may be visible. Turn here and the fun begins. After driving along a ranch road for a mile or so, a sign greets you, saying, "Livestock on the road ahead." Sure enough, a few turns later, horses and cows are feeding along the roadway and look up momentarily, unimpressed as you drive past them. A cluster of buildings can be seen on the right, and there on the left, the winery appears between the trees.

Ed Manigold, owner and winemaker, says it's unlikely that they will request a state winery sign for their establishment. Since the winery is located in a dry county, tours and tastings are permitted, but retail sales are not. The Manigolds will continue to offer group and individual tastings by special arrangement.

Built on a hillside at 900 feet above sea level, the winery is a beautiful architectural combination of strength and design. The 17.5 acre vineyard, undulating down the hill in front of the winery contains, Cabernet Sauvignon, Merlot, Chardonnay, Sauvignon Blanc, Zinfandel, Semillion, Muscat Blanc, and Johannisburg Riesling. From this vineyard, Ed and Madeleine produce fine estate bottled wines, including Cabernet Sauvignon, Chardonnay, Sauvignon Blanc, and a Texas Blush.

THE WINES

Bonded in 1995, Spicewood Vineyards released its first wine—a Holiday Blush—that same year and sold out in the first nine days. The following year it released a delicious Chardonnay and a Sauvignon Blanc, which were followed by two reds, a Merlot and a Cabernet Sauvignon in 1997. These red wines were produced with the surlies method and aged in French oak for eighteen months. The Chardonnay, an unfiltered wine, has won numerous awards since its release, including the prestigious Grand Harvest Award and a silver in the Lone Star Competition in 1996.

Dedicated to producing quality Hill Country wines, the Manigolds look forward to the future as their vineyard continues to mature, improving the fruit quality. As producers of handcrafted wines, the Manigolds understand the importance of the relationship between quality grapes and quality wines. They are hands-on owners who participate in every stage of the process, including planting and tending the vineyards, picking the grapes, making the wine and personally bottling it.

Though unavailable for sale at the winery, Spicewood wines are available in the Austin and Marble Falls areas.

DIRECTIONS: WE LEAVE THE AROMATIC SPICE BUSHES GROWING ALONG CYPRESS CREEK NEXT TO SPICEWOOD VINEYARDS FOR THE BEAUTY OF LAKE TRAVIS AND SLAUGHTER-LEFTWICH VINEYARDS. WE WILL TAKE SH 71 SOUTH TO FM 620 IN BEE CAVE AND TURN NORTH. BE PREPARED FOR SOME EXQUISITE VIEWS OF THE LAKE TRAVIS FROM THE DECKS OF THIS WINERY.

♣Slaughter-Leftwich Vineyards

107 RR 620 South, Box 22F, Austin, Texas 78732
Phone: (512) 266-3331, Fax: (512) 266-3180

OPEN 1–5 P.M.
THURSDAY–SUNDAY
TOURS: SATURDAY AND SUNDAY
ONLY

TASTINGS, RETAIL SALES,
AND GIFTS

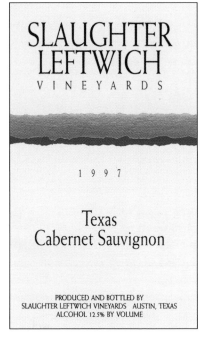

When planning a trip to the Hill Country, it is difficult not to include a visit to one of the many enjoyable water recreational areas. Just west of Austin is Lake Travis, offering water sports, restaurants, and a winery high in the hills that surround the lake—Slaughter-Leftwich Vineyards.

The Slaughter-Leftwich family opened this hillside winery in the fall of 1988 to process grapes from their west Texas vineyards. Years of observing other Texas wineries garner multiple awards for wines produced in their vineyards prompted the family to experiment with winemaking themselves. The Lake Travis location was selected for easy public access as well as a wonderful view of the lake near the Mansfield Dam.

The hillside winery is a magnificent native-stone facility, designed in the tradition of early Texas architecture. The tasting room is located on the second level of the winery to take advantage of the panoramic view of Lake Travis from the upper deck. Set high above the trees for an unobstructed view, the deck is an attractive setting for a wedding or other special occasions.

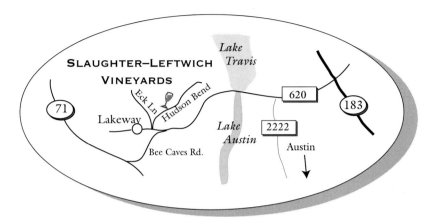

SLAUGHTER-LEFTWICH VINEYARDS

THE WINES

As you enter the winery, you are greeted by an acre of Merlot grapes planted as an experiment designed to test the rocky hillside growing conditions and also to add to the charm of the facility. Planted in 1993, these young vines will need at least eight years before they begin to produce wine-quality grapes.

Winemaker Scott Slaughter produces his wines using the high quality grapes from the family's 45-acre vineyard in West Texas. The vineyard includes Chardonnay, Chenin Blanc, Ruby Cabernet, Cabernet Sauvignon, and Petit Sirah grapes.

Slaughter-Leftwich Vineyards wines have won numerous awards such as Best of Show for their 1986 Chardonnay at the Houston Club Competition and a gold medal for their 1993 Sauvignon Blanc in the Tenth Annual Dallas Morning News Wine Competition.

The winery currently offers a rich Cabernet Sauvignon and a magnificent Chardonnay as their varietals. The "Austin" line of table wines includes Austin Blush, Austin Blanc, and Austin Rosé.

ENJOY A BREATHTAKING VIEW OF LAKE TRAVIS.
(COURTESY OF AUSTIN CONVENTION AND VISITORS BUREAU)

WHAT TO SEE IN THE AREA

After enjoying a tour of the Slaughter-Leftwich Vineyards, what better place to relax and enjoy a bottle of their wine than on the edge of picturesque Lake Travis? One of the famous Highland Lakes, this 18,930-acre lake winds between steep scenic hills for 65 miles and has some 270 miles of shoreline dedicated to camping, resorts, marinas, and leisure homes. This lake is tremendously popular for boating, skiing, sailing, fishing, mineral outcroppings and fossils. Lake fish records include Guadalupe bass –3.69 lb., striped bass–30.5 lb., and large mouth bass–8.75 lb.

For those of you who enjoy caverns, just take SH 620 to IH 35 and head north to Georgetown—the location of Inner Space, Texas' newest and most accessible cavern. Its subterranium beauty includes stalactites, floorstones, and the remains of prehistoric mastodons, wolves, and ice age animals.

DIRECTIONS: AFTER ENJOYING THESE WINES AND THE VIEW OF LAKE TRAVIS, WE HEAD SOUTH ON SH 71 TO SH 290, TURNING WEST TOWARD DRIPPING SPRINGS TO VISIT CANA CELLARS WINERY. FIVE MILES DOWN THE ROAD, YOU WILL SEE FITZHUGH ROAD AND A TEXAS WINERY SIGN. TURN HERE. APPROXIMATELY A HALF A MILE FARTHER WILL BE THE ENTRANCE TO CANA CELLARS.

❧Cana Cellars Winery

11217 Fitzhugh Road, Austin, Texas 78736
Phone: (512) 288-2582

OPEN 12–5 P.M.
SATURDAY–SUNDAY

(OTHER TIMES BY APPOINTMENT)

TOURS, TASTINGS,
AND RETAIL SALES

1996 Texas
Muscat Canelli

Vinted and bottled by Cana Cellars, Austin, Texas
10.0% by volume, BWN #98

The rugged rock-face of the Balcones Escarpment—the edge of a large uplift of land—towers above you as you glide along SH 290. As you approach Cana Cellars Winery, the edge of the escarpment plunges underground, leaving only the rolling landscape between Oak Hill and Dripping Springs.

Joe and Deena Turner, owners of Cana Cellars Winery, are blessed to be landowners in this picturesque area, where a chaotic geological past has given way to dramatic landscapes. As you pull into their farm off Fitzhugh Road, you are welcomed by the sight of longhorn steer casually grazing along the roadside. As you make your way up the curving one-lane blacktop leading up to the winery itself, a sign warns you: "Loose Livestock."

The winery is truly a cellar, having been built into the basement of a home already on the property when Joe purchased the land. As a lover of wine and a visitor to a friend's vineyard/winery in Italy over the years, the first thing Joe did was plant a two-and-a-half acre vineyard. Today the vineyard plays host to Cabernet Sauvignon, Sauvignon Blanc, Merlot, and Chardonnay grapes for the Cana Cellars wines.

The vineyard was in its fifth year when Joe and Deena married. As an incredibly romantic gesture, the Turners decided to release

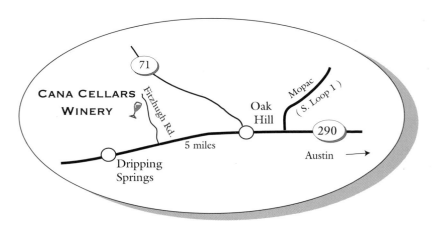

CANA CELLARS WINERY

their first wine for their wedding. Although, as Deena told us, bottling hundreds of bottles of wine hours before five hundred wedding guests were to arrive wasn't exactly a romantic experience. The wine was a success however, and both newlyweds proudly showed off the first release of Cana Cellars wines.

The winery, housed in the basement of their ranch home, is a charming combination of handcrafting and efficient use of space. Entering through massive rounded oak doors, you step directly into the barrel room/production facility of the winery. Another warmly lit room off to one side houses the tasting room. Here, beneath the low ceilings, the walls are handsomely lined with wine racks, storing all the wines available from Cana Cellars. Music fills the air as Joe or Deena proudly take you on a tasting tour of their wines. While there was no gift shop available during our visit, Deena explained that they will be expanding their offerings soon.

The Turners enlisted Enrique Ferro as their wine consultant. Enrique has a long history of experience in the Texas vineyards and is a consultant for a number of wineries around the state. Using the grapes of the Turner vineyard, along with grapes purchased from around the state, Cana Cellars produced approximately two-thousand cases of wine in its first year. Deena told us that while they don't plan to expand their production capability for a number of years, they will be expanding their selection.

In the fall of 1997, Cana Cellars offered a Fumé Blanc, Muscat Canelli, and a Cabernet Rose. The Rose won the People's Choice award at Grapefest '97, and the Muscat Canelli—made in the traditional Italian style—took the silver at two separate national competitions. Cana Cellars will soon release a Chardonnay, a Cabernet Sauvignon, and a Merlot.

While Cana Cellars was our last winery open to the public, we would be remiss if we did not include a discussion on Oak Hill Cellars, one of the more recent additions to the Texas wine industry. Though not open to the public, look for great things from this winery in the coming years.

❧Oak Hill Cellars

7512 Old Bee Caves Road, Austin, Texas 78735
Phone: (512) 288-2096

> WINERY IS NOT OPEN TO THE
> PUBLIC. THE WINES MAY BE
> PURCHASED AT RETAILERS IN THE
> OAK HILL AREA

Oak Hill Cellars is a new addition in the Texas wine industry that was started by Susan Benz and Brian Wilgus and bonded in 1995. They plan to produce a limited amount of two or three varietal wines. Their 1996 production was listed at 200 cases.

Wine trail adventurers should always be on the lookout for these types of operations. A small

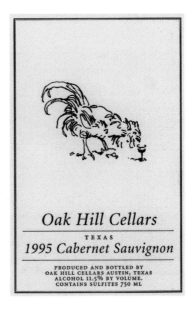

Oak Hill Cellars

TEXAS
1995 Cabernet Sauvignon

PRODUCED AND BOTTLED BY
OAK HILL CELLARS AUSTIN, TEXAS
ALCOHOL 11.5% BY VOLUME.
CONTAINS SULFITES 750 ML

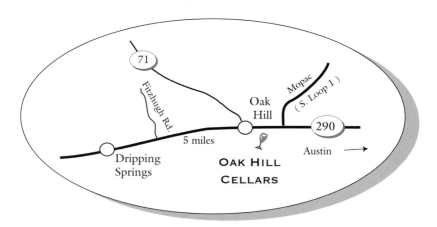

OAK HILL CELLARS WINERY

production is not a sign of lack of interest. A start-up operation with a clear focus on goals is always a good sign of quality products. This type of dedication and hard work will allow Susan Benz and Brian Wilgus to be major players in the wine industry in Texas.

When we spoke with Brian in the fall of 1997, he was humble—even hesitant—about appearing in this book. As a small-volume winery that is not open to the public, Brian felt his winemaking efforts were not yet important enough for publication. We couldn't disagree more. The courage and hard work exhibited by Susan and Brian underscore the tough pioneer spirit that has helped the Texas wine industry bounce back from adversity.

Oak Hill Cellars is the first winery to be established within the Austin city limits. Located on Old Bee Caves Road, it sells its wines through local grocery chains in the area. Look for Oak Hill Cellars to move in the future. Brian says they are looking for good vineyard land, and plan to establish their own vineyard and winery.

This is our last winery along the Highland Trail. We hope you have enjoyed your trip through the Hill Country wine trails.

Along the Trail

Austin, Travis, LBJ, Buchanan—no, not a list of statesmen—these names, along with Inks and Marble Falls, identify the six Highland Lakes that dominate the landscape along this trail. Water. Water everywhere, be it the cool, clear spring-fed streams or the deep blue beauty of these lakes, serves as a backdrop for life in this part of the Hill Country.

The Highland Lakes are popular during the summer, and visitors to the area can choose from fishing, hunting, boating, and even inner-tube rides down the rivers. Holidays can be crowded, so make plans in advance if you'll be visiting during one of the summer holiday weekends. This area is also a mecca for bravely going where none have gone before along winding two-lane roads through breathtaking scenes of the Hill Country. While always beautiful, Springtime is perhaps the most scenic.

The Highland Trail actually circles the Highland Lakes area. On the northern leg, you travel along well-paved, winding roads just made for a convertible and pass through a series of scenic and historic communities such as Jonestown and Marble Falls. The quarries around Marble Falls supplied the marble for the

TEXAS WINERIES OFTEN SCATTER VINEYARDS ACROSS THE STATE TO MINIMIZE HAIL DAMAGE. (COURTESY OF GRAPE CREEK VINEYARDS)

ENJOYING THE ROMANTIC SETTING OF A TEXAS TOWN ALONG THE WINE TRAIL. (COURTESY OF AUSTIN CONVENTION AND VISITORS BUREAU)

construction of the state capitol building in Austin. The town of Kingsland, located at the confluence of the Llano and Colorado rivers, is a popular fishing spot—and has been for centuries.

The southern leg of the trail is a more casual drive along SH 71. A straighter shot, the trip between Spicewood Vineyards and Slaughter-Leftwich will be less twisting and not as steep as you make your way back toward Austin. The city of Austin often feels like a big smalltown. As the state capital and host to prominent universities, Austin offers the charm of a college town combined with the sophistication of a state capital. While the town has grown dramatically over the past ten years, it still manages to retain its smalltown atmosphere that drew so many over the years.

Billing itself as the "Live Music Capital of the World," Austin has it all: blues, country/western, jazz, Tejano, and rock. The popular Sixth Street area is home to much of this entertainment along with a great selection of eateries.

Austin is also host to the Hill Country Wine and Food Festival every April. A major event that attracts Texas and California wineries, the event is a collage of dinners, luncheons, early morning and afternoon wine tastings, and desserts and food from some of the finest restaurants in Texas. The festival also includes musical guests, charitable auctions, and a black-tie extravaganza with a gourmet dinner and dancing into the night. A particular favorite of ours is the Lunch with the Vintners. Festival attendees are given a list of restaurants. They are asked to pick one and attend a luncheon there with mystery vintners. The mystery is the attendees do not know which winery or wineries will be represented until they arrive. We had the pleasure of sitting with vintners from Spicewood Vineyards and Becker Vineyards for a truly enjoyable lunch that once again confirmed our opinion that folks in the wine industry have to be some of the nicest people we have ever met.

If you are interested in this event, you can contact the festival's management at Texas Hill Country Wine and Food Festival, 1006 Mopac Circle, Ste. 102, Austin, TX 78746. The phone number is (512) 329-0770.

BED AND BREAKFASTS ALONG
THE ENCHANTED TRAIL

Boerne

BOERNE LAKE LODGE BED AND BREAKFAST RESORT

Hosts: Leah Glast and Alan Schuminsky, 310 Lakeview Drive, Boerne 78006, (210) 816-6060 or (800) 809-5050, also listed with Bed and Breakfast Hosts of San Antonio (800) 356-1605, 3 separate accommodations, continental and full breakfast, $$$$, no cr

OLDFATHER INN BED AND BREAKFAST

Host: Valerie Oldfather, 120 Old San Antonio Rd., Boerne 78009, (210) 249-8908, also listed with Bed and Breakfast Hosts of San Antonio (800) 356-1605, 2 cottages, OYO full breakfast, $$$–$$$$, no pets, smoking in designated areas, children 10 and over, MC, V, AE, DC

Comfort

BRINKMANN HOUSE BED AND BREAKFAST

Hosts: Melinda and John McCurdy, 714 Main Street, Comfort 78013, (210) 995-3141, 2 cottages with private baths, gourmet breakfast, $$, no pets, no children (with exceptions), smoking in restricted areas, phone in house, no cr

COMFORT COMMON

Hosts: Jim Lord and Bobby Dent, P.O. Box 539, Comfort 78013, (210) 995-3030, 5 rooms (ask about baths), 2 suites, 2 cottages (one a log cabin), unique breakfast arrangements, $$–$$$, TV in rooms, no children, smoking in restricted areas, all cr

THE MEYER BED AND BREAKFAST ON CYPRESS CREEK

Dorcas Mussett, Innkeeper, 845 High Street, P.O. Box 1117, Comfort 78013, (800) 364-2138 or (210) 995-2304, 9 suites with private baths, full breakfast, $$, cable TV, smoking outside, no pets, AE, MC, V

IDLEWILDE LODGE

Hosts: Hank and Connie Engle, 115 Texas Hwy. 473, Comfort 78013, (210) 995-3844, 2 cabins, full breakfast, $$, smoking in restricted areas, pets allowed, no cr

Dripping Springs

DABNEY HOUSE

Hosts: Jack and Patti Dabney, Autumn Lane, Dripping Springs, Wimberley Lodging Reservations, (800) 460-3909, room with king-sized bed and cottage suite with queen-sized bed, $$–$$$, smoking in restricted area, children accepted, no pets

SHORT MAMA'S HOUSE B&B

Host: Keely Peel, Manager, 101 College, Dripping Springs, (512) 858-5668, 4 bedrooms with baths (1 bedroom has an extra room with a twin bed), continental breakfast, $$–$$$, no smoking, no children, no pets, cr

Fredericksburg

ADMIRAL NIMITZ BIRTHPLACE AND
COUNTRY COTTAGE INN

Hosts: Michael and Jean Sudderth, 249 E. Main, Fredericksburg 78624, (210) 997-8549, 9 suites, gourmet breakfast, $$$–$$$$, no pets, no smoking, MC, V

AUSTIN STREET RETREAT

Unhosted: Contact Gastehaus Schmidt, (210) 997-5612, 5 separate quarters, OYO continental breakfast, $$$, no pets, children allowed, no smoking, all cr

BAETHGE-BEHREND HAUS

Unhosted: Contact Gastehaus Schmidt, (210) 997-5612, guest house with 2 bedrooms sleeps 6, 2 baths, OYO continental breakfast, $$$, children welcome, no pets, smoking outside only, all cr

BED AND BREW

Hosts: Richard Estenson and John Davies, The Fredericksburg Brewing Company, 245 E. Main, Fredericksburg 78624, (210) 997-1646, 12 rooms with private baths, brew in lieu of breakfast, $$–$$$, no pets, no children, smoking outside only, AE, V, MC

THE DELFORGE PLACE

Hosts: George and Betsy Delforge, Contact Gastehaus Schmidt, (210) 997-5612, 3 rooms, 3 baths, 1 suite, gourmet breakfast, $$–$$$, no pets, no children, no smoking, D, MC, V

FREDERICKSBURG BAKERY BED & BREAKFAST

Hosts: Mike and Patsy Penick, Contact Gastehaus Schmidt, (210) 997-5612, 3 suites, continental plus breakfast, $$$, no pets, no children, no smoking, D, MC, V

HILL COUNTRY GUESTHOUSE AND GARDEN

Unhosted: Contact Gastehaus Schmidt, (210) 997-5612, 2 suites, full breakfast or continental plus, $$$, no pets, no children, smoking outside in designated areas

HOTOPP HOUSE

Unhosted: Contact Gastehaus Schmidt, (210) 997-5612, 2 separate suites or entire house available, OYO continental plus, $$$$, children welcome, no pets, no smoking, all cr

MAGNOLIA HOUSE

Hostess: Joyce Kennard, 101 East Hackberry, Fredericksburg 78624, (210) 997-0306, fax (210) 997-0766, 4 rooms, 4 baths, 2 suites, full breakfast, $$–$$$, no pets, no children, smoking in common areas only, MC, V, AE

SCHMIDT BARN

Hostess: Loretta Schmidt. Contact Gastehaus Schmidt, (210) 997-5612, 1-bedroom barn, continental plus breakfast, $$, no restrictions, D, MC, V

THE YELLOW HOUSE AND THE KEEPSAKE KOTTAGE

Unhosted: Contact Gastehaus Schmidt, (210) 997-5612, both have queen-sized beds, OYO continental breakfast, $$–$$$, infants and children 12 and over, no pets, no smoking, all cr

WATKINS HILL GUEST HOUSE

Host: Edgar Watkins, 608 East Creek Street, Fredericksburg 78624, (800) 899-1672, (210) 997-6739, 2 suites, 2 log guest rooms, all with private baths, gourmet breakfast, $$$$, no pets, infants, or children over 12, smoking outside in designated areas, MC, V

Stonewall

HOME ON THE RANGE B&B

Hosts: Don and Velna Jackson (known locally as The Stonewall Jackson), Route 2721, Stonewall, (888) 458 BEVO, (800) 460-2380, (210) 644-2380, or contact Hill Country Accommodations (512) 847-5388, 1 cottage (sleeps 6), full breakfast in refrigerator, $$, 11 stocked ponds, Longhorn lean beef, 2 barbecue pits, no pets, restricted smoking, cr

RESTAURANTS ALONG THE ENCHANTED TRAIL

Boerne

BEAR MOON BAKERY AND CAFE

401 S. Main St., Boerne, (830) 816-2327, Soup/Sandwiches, Breakfast Buffet, Open Tuesday–Sunday for breakfast and lunch only, $

COUNTRY SPIRIT

707 S. Main St., Boerne, (830) 249-3607, Homestyle cooking, Beer and wine, Texas wines, Open Wednesday–Monday, $

FAMILY KORNER RESTAURANT

Highway 46, Boerne, (830) 249-3054, Homestyle cooking, Bar Open Monday–Sunday, $$

MARGARITA'S PATIO

1361 S. Main St., Boerne, (830) 249-9846, Mexican, Bar Open daily, $$

PEACH TREE KOUNTRY KITCHEN

448 S. Main St., Boerne, (830) 249-8583, Homestyle cooking, Open Thursday–Saturday for lunch only, $

PO-PO FAMILY RESTAURANT

435 NE IH 10 Access Rd., Boerne, (830) 537-4194 American, Beer and wine, Texas wines, Open Thursday–Sunday, $$

SCUZZI'S ITALIANO RISTORANTE

128 W. Blanco Rd., Boerne, (830) 249-8886, Italian, Bar, Texas wines, Open daily, $$–$$$

SUNSET GRILL

430 W. Bandera Rd., Boerne, (830) 816-2663, American, Beer and wine, Open daily, $$

Comfort

DOUBLE D CAFE

SH 27, west of the bridge, (830) 995-2001, American, Beer only, Monday–Saturday for breakfast, lunch, and dinner, breakfast only on Sunday, $

CYPRESS CREEK INN

400 block of SH 27, (830) 995-3977, American, Beer and St. Genevieve wines, Lunch and dinner Tuesday–Saturday, lunch only on Sunday, $

Dripping Springs

See Austin.

Fredericksburg

ALTDORF RESTAURANT

301 W. Main, Fredericksburg, (830) 997-7774, American-Mexican-German, Beer and wine, Lunch and dinner Wednesday–Monday, closed Tuesday and the month of January, $–$$

ANDY'S DINER

413 S. Washington/US 87, Fredericksburg, (830) 997-3744, American-German, Breakfast, lunch, dinner Tuesday–Saturday, Breakfast and lunch only Sunday–Monday, $

ENGEL'S DELI

320 E. Main, Fredericksburg, (830) 997-3176, Salads, soups, sandwiches, pastries, Breakfast and lunch Monday–Saturday, $

GEORGE'S OLD GERMAN BAKERY AND RESTAURANT

225 W. Main, Fredericksburg, (830) 997-9084, Salads, sandwiches, pastries, Breakfast, lunch and dinner Thursday–Monday, $

Stonewall

See Austin.

BED AND BREAKFASTS ALONG
THE HIGHLAND TRAIL

Austin

AUSTIN'S WILDFLOWER INN

Host: Kay Jackson, 1200 W. 22½ Street, Austin 78705, (512) 477-9639, fax (512) 474-4188, 4 guest rooms, 3 baths, full breakfast, $–$$, children welcome, but no smoking inside or pets, MC, V, AE

BREMOND HOUSE

Host: Connie Burton, 404 W. 7th, Austin 78701, (512) 482-0411, fax (512) 479-0789, 4 rooms, 2 private baths, 1 shared, gourmet breakfast, $$–$$$, no pets, smoking on porch or grounds only, MC, V

THE BROOK HOUSE

Host: Barbara Love, 609 W. 33rd, Austin 78705, (512) 459-0534, 6 guest rooms, 6 baths, full breakfast, $–$$, smoking on porches and grounds, all cr

CARRINGTON'S BLUFF AND THE GOVERNOR'S INN

Hosts: Lisa and Ed Mugford, 1900 David Street, Austin 78705, (512) 479-0638 or (800) 871-8908, fax (512) 476-4769, 8 rooms, 7 private baths, 1 shared, the Writers' Cottage, full breakfast, $–$$, children and (well-behaved) pets are welcome, but smoking outside only, all cr

CASA LOMA

Hosts: Ron and Sharon Hillhouse, 5512 Cuesta Verde, Austin 78746, (800) 222-0248 or (512) 327-7189, fax (512) 327-9150, 1 suite, 2 guest rooms, all private baths, full breakfast, $$$–$$$$, no children, pets, or smoking, all cr

CHEQUERED SHADE (LAKE AUSTIN)

Host: Millie Scott, 2530 Pearce Road, Austin 78730, (800) 577-5786 or (512) 346-8318, 3 rooms, 2 baths, full breakfast, $$, no pets or children under 12, smoking outside only, MC, V, AE

CITIVIEW

Host: Carol Hayden, 1405 E. Riverside Drive, Austin 78741,
(512) 441-2606 or (800) BST-VIEW, fax (512) 441-2949, 3 rooms,
3 baths, full breakfast, $$$, no smoking indoors, MC, V, AE

FAIRVIEW

Hosts: Duke and Nancy
Waggoner, 1304 Newning
Avenue, Austin 78704,
(512) 444-4746 or
(800) 310-4746, 4 rooms,
4 baths, 2 suites in the
Carriage House, full breakfast,
$$–$$$$, no pets or smoking,
children in Carriage House
only, all cr

THE GARDENS ON DUVAL

Host: Dorothy Sloan, 3210 Duval, Austin 78705, (512) 477-9200,
fax (512) 477-4220, 2 suites, full breakfast, $$, no children under 12,
pets, or indoor smoking, MC, V

THE INN AT PEARL STREET

Host: Jill Bickford, 809 West Martin Luther King at Pearl Street,
Austin 78701, (800) 494-2203 or (512) 477-2233,
fax (512) 795-0592, 5 guest rooms, private baths, continental
breakfasts OYO weekdays, full on Saturday, champagne brunch on
Sunday, $$$–$$$$, no children, pets, or smoking, all cr

LAKE TRAVIS BED AND BREAKFAST

Hosts: Judy and Vic Dwyer,
4446 Eck Lane, Austin
78734, (512) 266-3386,
3 bedrooms, 3 baths, full
breakfast, $$$$, no city hotel
tax, no children, pets, or
smoking inside, MC, V, AE

McCALLUM HOUSE

Hosts: Nancy and Roger Danley, 613 W. 32nd, Austin 78705, phone/fax (512) 451-6744, 3 guest rooms, 3 baths, 2 suites in Garden Apartment, full breakfast, $–$$$, no pets, but children over 11 are welcome, smoking on porches or grounds, MC, V

SOUTHARD-HOUSE

Hosts: Jerry and Rejina Southard, 908 Blanco, Austin 78703, (512) 474-4731, 4 rooms, 4 baths, 1 suite, 2 cottages, continental breakfast weekdays, full breakfast weekends with 3 seatings, $$–$$$, no pets, children, or smoking, all cr

WOODBURN HOUSE

Hosts: Herb and Sandra Dickson, 4401 Avenue D, Austin 78751, (512) 458-4335, 4 rooms, 4 baths, full breakfast, $$, children 9 and up, smoking on porches only, no pets, MC, V, AE

ZILLER HOUSE

Hosts: Sam and Wendy Kindred, 800 Edgecliff Terrace, Austin 78704, (800) 949-5446 or (512) 462-0100, fax (512) 462-9166, 3 rooms, private baths, 1 suite, Carriage House, full or continental breakfast OYO, $$–$$$, children welcome with prior approval, no pets, smoking on terraces only, MC, V, AE

Georgetown

CLAIBOURNE HOUSE

Host: Clare Easley, 912 Forest Street, Georgetown 78626, (512) 930-3934 and (512) 913-2272, 4 bedrooms, each with private bath (although 1 is on a separate floor), expansive continental breakfast, $$$, smoking in restricted area, children with prior arrangement, accommodates pets

THE HARPER-CHESSHER HISTORIC INN

Hosts: Leight Sumner Marcus; Manager: Kathy Frye, 1309 College Street, Georgetown 78628, (512) 863-4057, 4 rooms, 4 baths, buffet continental breakfast and noon high tea, $$$, no pets, no smoking, AE, MC, V

RIGHT AT HOME B&B

Host: Barbara Shepley, 1208 Main Street, Georgetown 78626-6727, (512) 930-3409 or (800) 651-0021, 4 rooms (2 with shared bath), full breakfast, dinners by request, $$, well-behaved children accepted, smoking outside, no TV in rooms (by design), MC, V

Lake Travis

CHANTICLEER LOG CABIN (SPICEWOOD)

Hosts: Ceaser and Mallonee Mellenger, P.O. Box 232, Spicewood 78669, (210) 693-4269 or ph/fax (512) 346-8814, 1 guest room, 1 bath, full breakfast, $$$, no pets, no children, smoking only on porch, no cr

TRAILS END

Hosts: JoAnn and Tom Patty, 12223 Trails End Rd. #7, Leander 78641, (512) 267-2901, (800) 850-2901, 2 guest rooms, 2 baths, 1 guest house, full breakfast, $–$$$, no pets, no smoking, MC, V

Luckenbach

LUCKENBACH INN B&B

Hosts: Capt. Matthew
Carinhas and Eva Carinhas,
HC 13, Box #9, Luckenbach
78624, (800) 997-1124,
(210) 997-2205, 6 rooms,
2 with Jacuzzis and fireplaces,
1 with shared bath downstairs,
gourmet breakfast, $$$,
no TV/phones in rooms,
accepts children and pets (with pet carriers), smoking in designated
areas, Saturday night dinners by reservation, wine cellar,
http://www.ccsi/~elyons/luckenbach.html

RESTAURANTS ALONG THE HIGHLAND TRAIL

Austin

BARBARA ELLEN'S

13129 SH 71 W. at RR 620, Austin, (512) 263-2385, American, Bar,
Texas wines, Lunch and dinner daily, $–$$

BASIL'S

900 W. 10th and Lamar, Austin, (512) 477-5576, Italian, Beer and
wine, Texas wines, Open daily, dinner only, $$$

CARMELO'S

504 E. 5th, Austin, (512) 477-7497, Italian, Bar, Texas wines, Open
daily, lunch and dinner, $$–$$$

CITY GRILL

401 Sabine, Austin, (512) 479-0817, Mesquite-grilled steak and
seafood, pasta, Bar, Texas wines, Dinner daily, $$

DAN MCKLUSKY'S

301 E. 6th, (512) 473-8924, or 10000 Research at the Arboretum,
(512) 346-0780, Austin, Steak, Bar, Texas wines, Dinner daily, Lunch
Monday–Friday on 6th St., Lunch daily at the Arboretum, $–$$

PEACOCKS ROAM THE WELL-MANICURED LAWNS WHILE GUESTS ENJOY VINTAGE SOUTHERN CUISINE AT GREEN PASTURES.

GREEN PASTURES

811 W. Live Oak, Austin, (512) 444-4747, American-Southern, Bar, Texas wines, Lunch and dinner Monday–Saturday, Brunch and dinner Sunday, $$–$$$$

HOT AND CRUNCHY TROUT IS A FAVORITE WITH DINERS AT HUDSON'S ON THE BEND.

HUDSON'S ON THE BEND

3509 RR 620, 1.5 miles southwest of Mansfield Dam, Austin, (512) 266-1369, Eclectic, Bar, Texas wines, Dinner daily, Reservations recommended, $$$

JEAN-PIERRE UPSTAIRS

3500 Jefferson at 35th, Austin, (512) 454-4811, Continental, Bar, Texas wines, Dinner Monday–Saturday, Lunch Monday–Friday, $$–$$$

THE WINE CELLAR AT JEFFREY'S HAS EARNED WINE SPECTATOR MAGAZINE'S AWARD OF EXCELLENCE EACH YEAR SINCE 1991. IT'S A FINE COMPLIMENT TO CHEF DAVID GARRIDO'S AWARD-WINNING TEXAS CUISINE.

JEFFREY'S

1204 W. Lynn, Austin, (512) 477-5584, Continental-Southwestern, Bar, Texas wines, Dinner Monday–Saturday, No reservations taken, $$–$$$

LA PALAPA

6640 US 290 East, Austin, (512) 459-8729, Tex-Mex, Bar, Texas wines, Open daily, lunch and dinner, $–$$

LOUIE'S 106

106 E. 6th, Austin, (512) 476-2010, Continental, Bar, Texas wines, Dinner daily, Lunch Monday–Friday, $–$$

ENJOY GOOD WINE AND GOOD FOOD ALONG THESE WINE TRAILS.
(COURTESY OF AUSTIN CONVENTION AND VISITORS BUREAU)

OLD PECAN STREET CAFÉ

310 E. 6th, Austin, (512) 478-2491, Continental, Bar, Texas wines, Lunch and dinner daily, $-$$

SHORELINE GRILL

98 San Jacinto in San Jacinto Center overlooking Town Lake, Austin, (512) 477-3300, Continental, Bar, Texas wines, Dinner daily, Lunch Monday–Friday, $$-$$$

THREADGILL'S

6416 N. Lamar, Austin, (512) 451-5440, American, Bar, Texas wines, Open daily, lunch and dinner, $

WEST LYNN CAFÉ

1110 West Lynn, (512) 482-0950, Continental, Beer and wine, Texas wines, Lunch and dinner daily, $

Z TEJAS GRILL

1110 W. 6th, (512) 346-3506 or 9400 Arboretum, Austin, (512) 478-5355, Southwestern, Bar, Texas wines, Breakfast, lunch, and dinner daily, Bar, Texas wines, $-$$

Georgetown

CROSETTI'S

119 West 7th, Georgetown, (512) 863-0596, American and Italian, Beer and wine, Texas wines, $-$$

Lake Travis

See Austin.

Luckenbach

See Austin.

Chapter 4

SOUTHEASTERN WINERIES

THE BRAZOS TRAIL

*I*f you decide to travel along SH 290 out of Houston on a sunny afternoon in mid-April to check out the annual display of bluebonnets, you will not be disappointed. As you near the town of Brenham, all along the road and up the hillsides you will see an explosion of blues, reds, and muted yellows, compliments of the Texas bluebonnet and Indian paintbrush wildflowers. Brenham has always been a treat for travelers, offering rolling hills, happy cows, the Blue Bell Ice Cream factory—a personal favorite. Now, Brenham even has a winery, and we are on our way to start the Brazos Trail.

The Brazos Trail, named for the Brazos River that dominates the area, will introduce you to five wineries: Pleasant Hill Winery, Messina Hof Wine Cellars, Wimberley Valley Winery, Red River Winery, and Piney Woods Country Wines. The Brazos Valley is an area as rich in history as the Brazos River is long, so leave enough time to do some sightseeing if you are a history buff.

As one of the shorter trails, it is ideal for a pleasant Saturday or weekday trip. You will pass through the towns of Brenham,

◀ CHARDONNAY AND CABERNET SAUVIGNON DOMINATE THE VINEYARDS IN TEXAS. (COURTESY OF THE TEXAS DEPARTMENT OF AGRICULTURE)

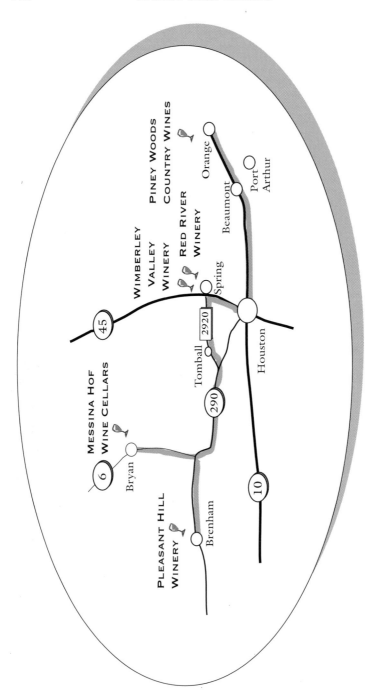

THE BRAZOS TRAIL WINERIES

> ## THE BRAZOS TRAIL
> ♣ Pleasant Hill Winery   ♣ Red River Winery
> ♣ Messina Hof Wine Cellars   ♣ Piney Woods Country Wines
> ♣ Wimberley Valley Winery

Bryan, Tomball, Old Town Spring, and Orange. These towns offer the weary traveler a wonderful selection of shops and restaurants to feed all of your urges.

Using Houston as your base, head north on SH 290 to Brenham—about an hour away, depending upon where you start in Houston. Turn left on SH 36 and within a mile you will spot a winery sign on the right side of the road, directing you to Pleasant Hill Winery on Salem Road. After enjoying the wine and hospitality of Bob and Jeanne Cottle, head back toward Houston. Traveling around twenty-two miles, turn left (north) on SH 6 to the town of Bryan, and you are ready to visit the ambiance of Old-World Italy at Messina Hof Wine Cellars. From

PAUL BONARRIGO, OWNER/WINEMAKER OF MESSINA HOF WINE CELLARS, PROUDLY DISPLAYS HIS AWARD-WINNING WINE.

Messina Hof, head back towards Houston, turning off SH 290 onto FM 2920, which will take you into Old Town Spring to visit Wimberley Valley Wines and Red River Winery. Each of these wineries fits well into Old Town Spring's exciting retail and dining atmosphere. After sampling the wines and stopping for a bite to eat, head south on IH 45 to IH 10 and eastward toward the city of Orange on the Texas-Louisiana border and a stop at Piney Woods Country Wines.

Now off to Pleasant Hill Winery!

✿Pleasant Hill Winery

1441 Salem Road, Brenham, Texas 77833
Phone: (409) 830-VINE, Fax: (281) 528-WINE

> **OPEN: 12–5 P.M.**
> **SATURDAY–SUNDAY**
>
> **TOURS, TASTINGS,**
> **RETAIL SALES, GIFTS**

After enjoying the ride in the country— perhaps even waving at a few of the happy Brenham cows, turn into the driveway of Pleasant Hill Winery, situated on forty acres of lushly covered rolling hills. The winery, built into the side of one of these rolling hills, was constructed from wood salvaged from the original structures that were there when Bob and Jeanne Cottle bought the property. A sturdy, rustic-looking structure, the hillside location allowed the Cottles to create a handsome cellar on the lower side to house the winemaking and fermentation facilities. But this is, after all, only phase one of their master plan.

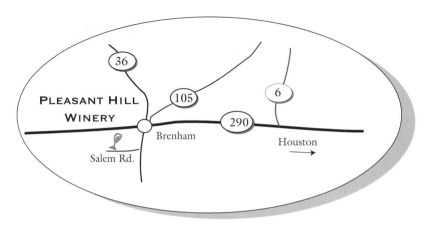

PLEASANT HILL WINERY

THE RUSTIC LOOK OF PLEASANT HILL WINERY IN BRENHAM.

Bob and Jeanne, both from Italian families with a long history of winemakers, have a vision. The Cottles describe a plan that includes another structure capable of holding up to 100,000 gallons, a maze of tunnels to pipe wine between buildings, a lake to

STEP THROUGH THESE DOORS FOR A TEXAS WINE ADVENTURE.

picnic alongside, and the largest crushing pad in Texas at 10,000 square feet. Quite a leap in scale for a couple who have been making only 200 gallons of wine in their Spring home.

As amateur winemakers since moving to Texas in the 1970s, the Cottles have been very active in amateur winemaking organizations in Texas—sharing what they have learned. In 1989 the couple decided to turn their passion into a way of life for their family. After making the decision to become a professional winemaker, Bob obtained his degree in oenology from Grayson County College in Denison, Texas, traveling over 300 miles each weekend for three years to earn the degree. When asked how the education will change the winemaking style he has used as a home winemaker, Bob said, "It has given me a much better technical understanding of the chemistry of wine." He feels it has vastly improved his winemaking techniques.

The equipment Bob bought from the Guadalupe Valley Winery when it closed its doors in the town of Gruene, sits below, waiting for grapes to ferment. The vineyard is too immature to produce quality grapes, and the Cottles have had difficulty finding surplus grapes or juice this year. Bob points to his vineyard and admits that it is one great experiment. East of IH 35, which is approximately where the humidity line is in Texas, the environment is harsh for grapes. The vineyard at Pleasant Hills is an experiment to find a grape that will survive both the disease and the heat and humidity.

The acre vineyard contains Black Spanish and Herbemont, both of which are known to do well in this environment, and a red grape called Cynthiana. Other vineyard rows include Champanel, Blanc DuBois, which could produce a sparkling wine, and Favorite, a grape native to the Brenham area. The favorite grape, once grown by the Niderauer Winery, which existed here from 1880s to the 1950s, is a hybrid of Black Spanish and Herbemont.

Pleasant Hill Winery has a well-stocked gift shop offering wines, wine accessories, and gifts. Outside the tasting room is a balcony that offers a fantastic view of the undulating property. The existing vineyard, visible from the balcony, will be expanded by an acre a year and should provide a dramatic view from this perch.

The wines Bob prefers are made in the French style of winemaking, similar to Becker Vineyards' technique.

From his experimental vineyard, he will use the Cynthiana to produce a Cabernet Sauvignon-style wine, and create a sparking wine from the Blanc Dubois grapes. Of course, he will have to wait a few years for the vines to mature enough for wine-quality grapes. In the meantime, Bob admits to being at the mercy of whatever grapes he can find. He would soon like to offer a selection of sweet wines and tables wines such as Calena Rose and Calena Bianca.

With the passion this family has for winemaking, we can expect great things from the Pleasant Hills Winery in years to come.

DIRECTIONS: FROM PLEASANT HILL WINERY RETURN TO SH 290, AND HEAD EAST BACK TOWARD HOUSTON TO SH 6, WHICH IS ABOUT 22 MILES AWAY. TURN NORTH ONTO SH 6 TOWARD THE CITY OF BRYAN, USUALLY REFERRED TO AS BRYAN-COLLEGE STATION BECAUSE THE TWO TOWNS MERGE TOGETHER AND HAVE TEXAS A&M UNIVERSITY AS THEIR ANCHOR. MESSINA HOF WINE CELLARS IS THE NEXT STOP ON OUR TOUR—ONE THAT IS GOING TO BE A REAL TREAT FOR WINE AND FOOD LOVERS ALIKE.

♣Messina Hof Wine Cellars

4545 Old Reliance Road, Bryan, Texas 77808
Phone: (409) 778-9463, Fax: (409) 778-1729

TOURS: 1:00 AND 2:30
MONDAY–FRIDAY; 11 A.M., 12:30,
2:30 AND 4:00 P.M. SATURDAY;
12:30 AND 2:30 SUNDAY

TASTINGS, RETAIL SALES, GIFTS,
RESTAURANT, AND BED
AND BREAKFAST

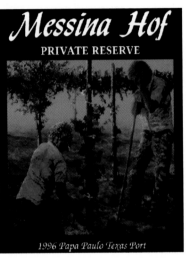

Messina Hof
PRIVATE RESERVE

1996 Papa Paulo Texas Port

Family, tradition and romance—three fundamental elements that have shaped Paul and Merrill Bonarrigo's approach to winemaking in Texas. Located in the town of Bryan, the Messina Hof Wine Cellars is an award-winning winery, enjoying recognition in the United States, Europe, and Japan.

A visit to the Messina Hof winery (only 90 miles from Houston) is a pleasant two-and-a-half hour drive on SH 6. In the spring the traveler is treated to vistas of rolling hills covered with bluebonnets and Indian paintbrushes. In the fall, the landscape is cloaked in the autumn colors of the hardwood trees. You can plan a trip with just the winery tour in mind, or visit the winery and enjoy a picnic with the wine you purchase. With the variety of sights and activities available in the valley, the only thing difficult about this short jaunt will be deciding what to do.

Paul's winemaking skills are a combination of the Old World traditions taught to him by his grandmother and his education from the Napa Wine School at the University of California at Davis. Here he learned that when his grandmother taught him to use his senses to determine tartness and sweetness, he was actually evaluating the acidity and sugar in the wine.

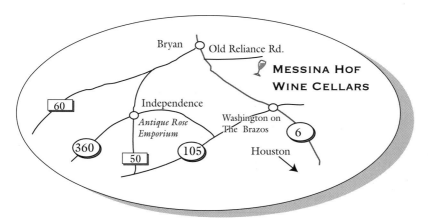

Bryan

Old Reliance Rd.

MESSINA HOF
WINE CELLARS

60

Independence

Antique Rose Emporium

Washington on The Brazos

360

50

105

Houston

6

MESSINA HOF WINE CELLARS

The winery's name, Messina Hof, combines the name of the European towns that were the origins of Paul's and Merrill's families—Messina, Sicily, and Hof, Germany. Their tradition of winemaking goes back two hundred years, when Paul's grandfather made wine for the people in his village. That tradition continued when the Bonarrigos moved to New York's Little Italy in 1927. In the Bonarrigo family, the first son is always named Paul and is given the responsibility of being the winemaker for his generation. The Messina Hof vintner, Paul V, is the first Bonarrigo to produce and sell wine commercially in the United States.

The tasting room, a romantic country affair with a warming fireplace when a chill reaches the Bryan area, offers a splendid collection of gifts, accessories, and foods, including cheeses. During pleasant weather, the Bonnarigos encourage folks to take a hunk of cheese along with one of their bottles of wine out to the deck overlooking their small lake.

The original bed and breakfast on the grounds of the winery will soon be replaced by a larger facility to accommodate the increased demand by visitors who want to spend a romantic weekend at Messina Hof. Book ahead though; there is usually a waiting list for this charming hideaway. A special event takes place every November, when the Bonarrigos celebrate the release of the new wines with a grand dinner and a ceremony that presents a Texas artist an award for a new wine label design.

A recent addition is the restaurant and conference center, which has become very popular with local residents. Paul's chef prepares a wonderful selection of foods for evening dinner and for special occasions such as weddings in the comfortable restaurant with the look and feel of a wine cellar. Don't be surprised to see the master vintner walking around this premier restaurant to greet his guests on any given evening. Because of Texas laws, the restaurant is unable to sell wine. Not to worry, though, simply stop at the tasting room and pick up a Messina Hof wine that you think would go with your meal that evening.

THE WINES

Paul and Merrill took a cautious approach to expanding their vineyard, working the land personally until the winery's vineyard reached thirty acres. Messina Hof recently expanded its facilities, and now harvests grapes from an additional 200 acres in Texas. Paul prefers to produce his reds in the Bordeaux style, while he

MESSINA HOF WINE CELLARS IN BRYAN.

THE WELL APPOINTED TASTING ROOM AT MESSINA HOF WINE CELLARS.

admires the German winemaking techniques for his white wines. In 1997, Paul introduced the concept of double-barrel fermentation for his wines. After the normal barrel fermenting Messina Hof has always used, Paul removes the wine and places it into a fresh oak barrel to extract that little extra something that make his wines so distinctive.

Messina Hof now produces eighteen different wines ranging from their Traditions label of table wines to their Private Reserve line including Cabernet Sauvignon and Papa Paulo Port. When asked to name the favorite of all his wines, Paul chose the Papa Paulo Port, made in honor of his father, as his signature wine. Three generations of Pauls are shown on the label.

The Messina Hof Winery has an active calendar of special events planned throughout the year. There are harvest weekends in which you can join their "Picker's Club" and participate in the picking of the grapes and in grape stomping. A tour of the after-harvest process and a sampling of wines produced from the previous harvest make the day complete. Other events include demonstration of vine grafting and a special dinner centered around fine meals with complementing Messina Hof wines.

Call for the latest planned events and schedules. Messina Hof has one of the most active events schedules in the state.

DIRECTIONS: FROM YOUR ENJOYABLE STAY AT MESSINA HOF, HEAD BACK
TO THE HOUSTON AREA TO VISIT TWO UNIQUE WINERIES. YOU WILL
RETRACE YOUR STEPS DOWN SH 6 TO SH 290, HEADING SOUTH TOWARD
HOUSTON. NEAR HOUSTON, TURN EAST ON FM 2920, WHICH WILL TAKE
YOU THROUGH THE TOWN OF TOMBALL YON OUR WAY TO OLD TOWN
SPRING. THE CITY OF TOMBALL HAS GROWN FROM A QUAINT TEXAS
TOWN TO A THRIVING METROPOLIS IN THE SHADOW OF HOUSTON. KNOWN
FOR ITS ANTIQUE STORES, IT OFFERS A VARIETY OF PLACES TO GRAB A
LUNCH BEFORE HEADING OFF TO OLD TOWN SPRING, WHICH IS
APPROXIMATELY A HALF HOUR AWAY.

OUR FIRST STOP IN OLD TOWN SPRING WILL BE WIMBERLEY VALLEY
WINERY. UPON ENTERING OLD TOWN SPRING, STAY LEFT AT THE FORK
IN THE ROAD.

☙Wimberley Valley Winery

206 Main Street, Old Town Spring, Texas 77373
Phone: (281) 350-8801

> TASTING ROOM HOURS:
> 11 A.M.–5 P.M.
> TUESDAY–SATURDAY;
> 12–5 P.M. SUNDAY

WIMBERLEY VALLEY WINES

Christmas Cuvee
WHITE WINE
TEXAS
ALC 12.0% BY VOL • 750 ML

Main Street in Old Town Spring is alive with music, colors, restaurants and people. Folks from all around stop here to shop, have a meal, or just people watch. Rising above all this activity on Main Street is a huge oak barrel, larger than a man is tall. This barrel marks the location of the Wimberley Valley Tasting Room. The winery itself is in Wimberley, Texas, and is located in a dry county. Dean Valentine, co-owner and winemaker, decided to open a tasting room in Old Town Spring to allow the public to sample his wine. Dean shares a building with his wife who specializes in Christmas decorations and takes up the right side of the building.

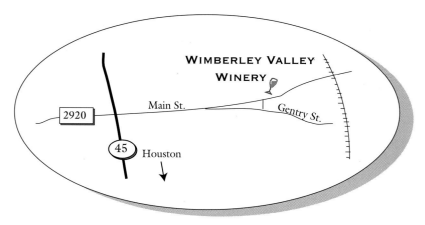

WIMBERLEY VALLEY WINERY

Dean began his career as a carpenter and home winemaker. In the 1970s Dean became involved with Guadalupe Valley Winery in Gruene, Texas. Eventually, he and a partner purchased the winery from its original owners and produced small quantities of a variety of Texas wines. The popularity of their wines convinced Dean to open his own winery in order to produce greater volumes of wine. In 1983, Wimberley Valley Winery was established on property Dean owned in the town of Wimberley. Shortly after producing his first wines, Dean established the Old Town Spring Tasting Room.

After four years of producing award-winning Chardonnay, Chenin Blanc, and Cabernet Sauvignon, Dean returned to the vision he originally had when building the winery. As he tells it, "In those early years, we all thought we had to be like California—make wine like California did. Well in those first few years, reality showed us that maybe that wasn't the case. Maybe we should be more like a Missouri or an Ohio winery."

THE WINES

As a winemaker in a young wine state, Dean realized he had to change his strategy in order to survive. The basis for the new direction came directly from comments of his customers in the tasting room. Many customers were unfamiliar with wine, or had sampled Texas wine and didn't like it. Dean realized these customers probably sampled a drier wine, which someone new to wine would not find to be pleasant tasting. At the same time, he noticed that his stock of Port consistently sold out.

GRAPES AFTER HARVEST—JUICY, PLUMP AND READY FOR THE PRESS. (COURTESY OF THE TEXAS DEPARTMENT OF AGRICULTURE)

A new line of wines called Texas Country Cellars was created, offering a red, blush, and white wine. Slightly sweeter than the traditional wines, they were an instant success with customers in the tasting room and through his distributors. Dean had found a large untapped market of wine consumers and, to this day, consistently sells all the wine he produces.

Wimberley Valley Winery continues to produce traditional wines as well. Its current production includes more Chardonnay, Chenin Blanc, and Cabernet Sauvignon that in recent years. His current annual production is around 6,000 cases, a third of which is classic wines. The future may see a small increase in production capacity, but as Dean puts it, "I never want to go beyond 100,000 gallons. It would become too unmanageable for me." Look for Wimberley Valley to continue a small selection of very good wines at a fair price.

DIRECTIONS: AFTER SAMPLING THESE FINES WINES, YOU MAY WISH TO CONTINUE TO ENJOY YOUR STAY IN OLD TOWN SPRING WHERE YOU CAN DO SOME SHOPPING OR GRAB A BITE TO EAT FROM ONE OF THE QUAINT RESTAURANTS. AFTER ALL, THE NEXT AND LAST WINERY ON THIS TRAIL, RED RIVER WINERY, IS JUST A FEW BLOCKS AWAY!

❧Red River Winery

421 Gentry Street #204, Old Town Spring, Texas 77373
Phone: (281) 288-WINE, Fax: (281) 362-9606

OPEN: 12–5 P.M.
TUESDAY–SUNDAY

TASTINGS, RETAIL SALES,
AND GIFTS

You won't find a vineyard around the Red River Winery in Old Town Spring, at least not yet. What you will find are the smiling faces of Mark and Tina Woolington welcoming you into their establishment. Red River's tasting room and gift shop is housed in a unique octagonal-shaped tower, giving the winery a distinctive character from the other retail shops in this cluster of buildings. It is a spacious place with a soaring ceiling, and its many windows fill the central area with sunshine to produce a bright, cheerful atmosphere. If you thought wineries had to be dark and damp, you are in for a pleasant surprise.

The Woolingtons path to becoming winery owners took them on a route that involved leaving mainland United States for an island adventure. After establishing themselves as players in the banking and real estate industries of Hawaii, Mark and Tina decided to move back to the mainland to be closer to family. Having come from a winemaking family, Mark and his brother saw Old Town Spring as a great environment to establish a small boutique winery. The rest, as they say, is history.

Bonded in 1995, Red River opened its doors in October of that year and offered a selection of gifts, handmade wine accessories, and, at first, only wines from other Texas wineries. Before its first anniversary neared, however, Red River was producing small quantities of its own wines. To date, Mark and Tina have released a Sauvignon Blanc, Cabernet Sauvignon, and a Blush. Each vintage is usually limited to approximately 120 gallons, so

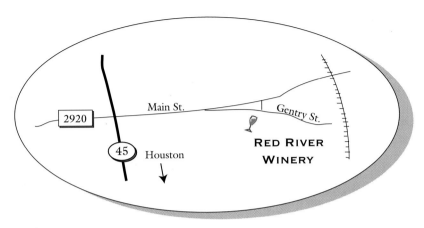

RED RIVER WINERY

if you enjoy what you taste on your visit, best buy it right then; it will probably be gone the next time you visit.

Mark, an easygoing man with a quick smile, was quite demur when we asked him about his winemaking technique. "I'm really still learning the craft of winemaking," he said. His early attempts at winemaking belie his genuine humility, however. The Sauvignon Blanc we tasted was a delightful surprise, exhibiting characteristics of the smokey, buttery tastes of a Chardonnay that had undergone secondary barrel fermentation. A recent Cabernet Sauvignon was also a grand surprise, with complex flavors of oak, spices, and berries. As Mark poured a sample of this wine, he simply offered, "We're fairly proud of this one." As indeed they should be.

Red River offers customers specialized labels on their wine. Customers can walk in, order a custom label, do some shopping around Old Town Spring, and pick up their customized wine afterward. Look for their specialized label offerings in major grocery chains such as Krogers and Albertsons. Shoppers will be able to fill out a label request form, then return to the store in five days to pick up their wine.

Whenever Mark is busy in the background working his label magic, Tina greets customers in their tasting room. Tina offers tastings of their own wine as well as wines from other Texas wineries. She will also be happy to help you select from one of the many wine-related food items they offer or explain one of the wine accessories she has handmade.

Future plans call for expanding the production and special functions capability of the facility. The backroom of the existing facility, which contains the fermenting and bottling areas, is used to host special functions for small groups. This area will be expanded into a barrel room capable of hosting larger groups for vintner dinner and small weddings.

The winery also offers outside seating in the small square that serves as a focal point for the numerous neighboring shops. During most of the year, live music is offered in the square on weekends. Mark and Tina invite you to buy a glass or bottle of wine, walk down the steps of the deck that opens onto the square, and sit under a tree-shaded table to enjoy the sounds and sights.

DIRECTIONS: FROM OLD TOWN SPRING YOU HAVE A CHOICE: THE FAST UNSCENIC WAY ALONG IH 10 OR THE SLOWER, SCENIC ROUTE ALONG FM 1960, WHICH BECOMES SH 90 AS IT NEARS THE CITY OF BEAUMONT. EITHER WAY, THE CITY OF ORANGE, TEXAS, IS APPROXIMATELY 100 MILES TO THE EAST.

❧Piney Woods Country Wines

3408 Willow Drive, Orange, Texas 77632
Phone: (409) 883-5408

OPEN: 9–5:30 P.M.
MONDAY–SATURDAY;
12:30–4 P.M. SUNDAY

TOURS BY APPOINTMENT ONLY

TASTINGS, RETAIL SALES,
AND GIFTS

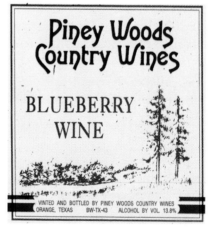

As you approach the city of Beaumont, the grand pines of Big Thicket National Preserve loom to the north and the damp organic scent of the forest can be detected as you drive along to the border town of Orange. Orange, the last stop along IH 10 in

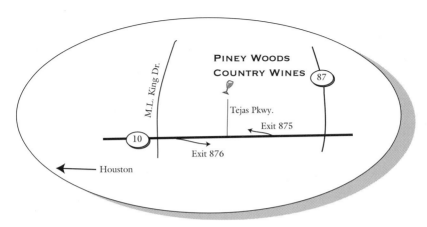

PINEY WOODS COUNTRY WINES

east Texas, is a portal to the southern states and home to Piney Woods Country Wines.

Piney Woods Country Wines specializes in Texas fruit and muscadine wines, under the watchful eye of Alfred Flies, owner and winemaker. In this part of Texas, the muscadine grape is king, as Alfred explains, "It's the only grape that will thrive around here." Pierce's disease and black rot lurk about, precluding the growth of vinifera grape varieties. Alfred is having good results from an experimental half acre of the Lenoir grapes and plans to expand this crop for production of his popular Port wine.

What started out as a hobby after retirement from interior design has become a big business over the past twelve years. Business has doubled recently, providing the catalyst for the latest round of expansions to the facility, vineyards, and orchards. Piney Woods grows all its own plums for it's popular Plum Wine, and uses local fruit for its Blueberry and Strawberry wines.

THE WINES

The style of wines Alfred produces is controlled primarily by his location in the state. His winery is too far east and south to grow vinifera or transport grapes or juice in from the rest of the state. Besides, as Alfred explains, he prefers to produce wines that reflect the local community and resources.

VISITORS ARE ENCOURAGED TO TAKE A WALKING TOUR AROUND PINEY WOODS COUNTRY WINES.

From his two-acre muscadine vineyard, Alfred produces six or seven wines, including two reds, a blush, and a white table wine. Depending on the harvest in any given year, the quantity of grapes and fruit will determine exactly what selection of wines he will make. In one particularly good harvest, Alfred had an excess of muscadine juice that he turned into his now famous Pecan Mocha Wine. Not exactly a dessert wine, nor a mead, it has a flavor unique unto itself. Oddly enough, the wine has become so popular over the past few years, Piney Woods has had to expand its muscadine vineyard to assure a plentiful supply of juice to keep producing this wine.

Piney Woods Country Wines offers two Port wines, the standard Port that Alfred has long produced, plus a lighter version that he calls Ports of Texas. With only fourteen percent alcohol content, this Port can be sold by establishments limited to offering products with an alcohol content under fourteen percent. With a lighter flavor, this Port outsells his regular Port in many markets and at the winery. Alfred's Port is also available in the tasting room of Wimberley Valley Wines in Old Town Spring.

What's in store for the future? According to Alfred, more of the same. As he puts it, "I'm going to leave the Cabs and the Chardonnays to my neighbors to the west." Alfred is happy to concentrate on his specialty wines that are unique in the Texas wine industry.

ALONG THE TRAIL

For travelers planning one-day trips, a tour of the wineries near Brenham can be combined with a stopover at the Antique Rose Emporium near the town of Independence on FM 50, just south of the intersection with FM 390. If you have a love for roses, this is a must see. The Emporium has created an English garden with many species of antique roses, native shrubs, and perennials. Its Fall Festival of Roses (usually planned for the first weekend in November) is filled with seminars and lectures on collecting and growing roses. There is a gift shop area with one-of-a-kind garden gifts and books. Ask them about their Republic of Texas Collection representing a collection of roses known to have grown when Texas was a republic. Also, their orphaned roses (roses that have lost their tags) usually come in grabbags at a great price. You can contact them at 409-836-9051 to request a mail-order catalog to browse before you visit.

Texas history can be seen at Washington on the Brazos State Park. Within this park you will also be able to visit the Star of Republic Museum, Independence Hall, and the Anson Jones House. All of these exhibits show early Texas life in one of the state's most picturesque parks and features picnic areas amidst rolling acres and live oaks. This is the site of the signing of the Texas Declaration of Independence. It wouldn't be hard to find a perfect spot for a romantic picnic in this park. A blanket, a crust of bread, a bottle of wine along the banks of the Brazos just could be the reason Sam Houston fought so hard for Texas.

Closer to Houston, the city of Tomball offers shopping and refreshments and a quaint cluster of antique stores to browse in along FM 2920. Further along the trail, Old Town Spring is a pure delight for adults and children, with restaurants, shops, shade trees to rest under with a cool drink, and even a Christmas store that is open all year. Old Town Spring is also well-known for its popular festivals held during the year, including the Crawfish Festival that features music, food, and fun, and the extremely popular Home For The Holidays Festival held every weekend in November and December.

For those wine tourists who venture out to Piney Woods Country Winery, the city of Orange is the easternmost city on the Sabine River boundary with Louisiana. Orange was established in 1836, the year of Texas Independence and was named after the wild orange groves on the banks of the Sabine. Downtown Orange offers marvelous walking tours and opportunities to sit and rest a spell with a cool drink before heading home.

BED AND BREAKFASTS ALONG THE BRAZOS TRAIL

Brenham

ANT STREET INN
BED AND BREAKFAST

Hosts: Tommy and Pam Traylor,
107 West Commerce, Brenham 77833,
(800) 481-1951, (409) 836-7393,
fax (409) 836-7595, 14 rooms with
private baths, gourmet breakfast, $$$–$$$$,
children over 12 welcome, no pets, smoking
in designated areas only, most cr

CAPTAIN TACITUS T. CLAY
HOUSE

Hosts: Thelma M. Zwiener,
Fieldstone Farm, 9445 FM 390
E. Independence, Brenham 77833,
(409) 836-1916, 5 guest rooms,
4 baths, full breakfast, $–$$,
children welcome, no pets, smoking
in designated areas, no cr

FAR VIEW—
A BED AND BREAKFAST

Hosts: David and Tonya Meyer,
1804 South Park Street, Brenham 77833,
(409) 836-1672, 5 bedrooms, 4 with private
baths, gourmet breakfast, $$$–$$$$,
children over 12 welcome, no pets, smoking
permitted in designated areas, MC, V, AE

SCHUERENBERG HOUSE

Host: Kay Gregory, 503 West Alamo, Brenham 77833,
(409) 830-7054, (800) 321-6234, 3 bedrooms (2 with private baths),
1 double suite, third-floor grand attic suite with private bath, gourmet
breakfast, $$$–$$$$, children over 12 welcome, no pets, smoking
permitted in designated areas, MC, V

JAMES WALKER HOMESTEAD

Hosts: John & Jane Barnhill, Route 7, Box 7176, Brenham 77833,
(409) 836-6717, fax (409) 836-6922, 1 bedroom, 1 loft, 1 daybed,
1 bath, full breakfast, $$$$, OYO, no pets, no children, no smoking, no cr

Bryan-College Station

ANGELSGATE
BED AND BREAKFAST

Hosts: Gary and Beth Goyen, 615 East 29th St., Bryan 77803, (409) 779-1231 or (888) 779-1231, 2 suites with private baths, gourmet breakfast, $$$–$$$$, children 10 and over welcome, no pets, smoking permitted outside only, MC, V

BONNIE GAMBREL (BRYAN)

Hosts: Blocker and Dorothy Trant, 600 East 27th St., Bryan 77803, (409) 779-1022, fax (409) 779-1040, 1 suite with private bath, 2 guest rooms, 1 bath, gourmet breakfast or brunch, $$$–$$$$, children 12 and over (facilities for one infant), no pets, smoking permitted in designated areas, MC, V, D

MESSINA HOF VINEYARD/VINTNER'S
LOFT BED & BREAKFAST (BRYAN)

Hosts: Paul & Merrill Bonarrigo, 4545 Old Reliance Rd., Bryan 77802, (409) 778-9463, fax (409) 778-1729, 1 bedroom, 1 bath, continental breakfast, $$$, no pets, no children, no smoking, MC, V, AE

THE FLIPPEN PLACE
(COLLEGE STATION)

Hosts: Flip and Susan Flippen, 1199 Haywood Dr., College Station 77845, (409) 693-7660, fax (409) 693-8458, 3 guest rooms, 3 private baths, gourmet breakfast, $$$–$$$$, no children, no pets, no smokers, MC, V, AE

Chappell Hill

BROWNING PLANTATION

Hosts: Richard and Mildred Ganchan, Route 1, Box 8, Chappell Hill 77426, (409) 836-6144, (713) 661-6761, 4 guest bedrooms, 2 private baths, 2 shared half baths, gourmet breakfast, $$$$, no pets, no children, no smoking, no cr

THE MULBERRY HOUSE

Host: Katie Cron, P.O. Box 5, Chappell Hill 77426, (409) 830-1311, 5 bedrooms, 5 baths, gourmet breakfast, $$–$$$, no pets, no children, no smoking, no cr

THE STAGECOACH INN

Hosts: Mr. and Mrs. H. Moore, Main at Chestnut, P.O. Box 339, Chappell Hill 77426, (409) 836-9515, 6 bedrooms, 4 baths, gourmet breakfast, $$$–$$$$, no pets, no children, no smoking, no cr

Houston

ANGEL ARBOR BED AND BREAKFAST INN

Host; Marguerite Swanson, 848 Heights Blvd., Houston 77007, (713) 868-4654, fax (713) 861-3189, 3 guest rooms, 1 suite, private baths, full breakfast, $$$$, no children, no pets, no smoking, MC, V, DC, AE

SARA'S BED AND BREAKFAST

Host: Donna and Tillman Arledge, 941 Heights Blvd., Houston 77008, (800) 593-1130, (713) 868-1130, fax (713) 868-1160, 10 bedrooms, 9½ baths, continental, $–$$, no pets, children in carriage house, smoking designated areas, all cr

Old Town Spring

McLACHLAN FARM BED AND BREAKFAST

Hosts: Jim & Joycelyn McLachlan Clairmonte, 24907 Hardy Road, (mailing address) P.O. Box 538, Spring 77383, (800) 382-3988, (713) 350-2400, 3 bedrooms, 2 baths, gourmet breakfast, $$–$$$$, no pets, no children, no smoking, no alcoholic beverages, please, no cr

RESTAURANTS ALONG THE BRAZOS TRAIL

Brenham

THE GREAT ANT STREET RESTAURANT

205 S. Baylor, Brenham, (409) 830-9060, American, Bar, $–$$

K & G STEAKHOUSE

2209 S. Market near Becker Dr., Brenham, (409) 836-7950, Breakfast, lunch, and dinner Tuesday–Sunday, dinner only Monday, Steak, seafood, chicken, Bar, $–$$

Bryan-College Station

BLACK FOREST INN

On TX 30 approx. 21 miles east of College Station, Bryan, (409) 874-2407, American-German, Beer and wine, Texas wines, dinner Wednesday–Saturday, Reservations required, $$

THE KAFFEE KLATSCH

106 North Ave., Bryan, (409) 846-4360, American, Lunch Monday–Saturday, $

THE TEXAN

3204 S. College, Bryan, (409) 822-3588, Continental, Bar, Texas wines, dinner Monday–Saturday, Reservations suggested, $$–$$$$

Chappell Hill

See Bryan-College Station.

Houston

BABA YEGA

2607 Grant, Houston, (713) 522-0042, American, Bar, Texas wines, Lunch and dinner daily, Breakfast Saturday–Sunday, $

BISTRO LANCASTER

701 Texas, Houston, (713) 228-9502, Steak, seafood, pasta, Bar, Texas wines, Reservations recommended, $$$$

BISTRO LANCASTER, LOCATED INSIDE THE LUXURIOUS LANCASTER HOTEL, IS AN EXCELLENT SPOT TO ENJOY A PRE-THEATER DINNER.

BRENNAN'S

3300 Smith, Houston,
(713) 522-9711, French-
Creole-Southwestern, Bar,
Texas wines, Lunch and
dinner Monday–Friday,
Brunch and dinner
Saturday-Sunday,
Reservations required,
$$$–$$$$

CHEF ROBERT DEL GRANDE'S FLAVOR-
CHARGED DISHES SUCH AS BEEF FILET
WITH MOLE SAUCE AND LOBSTER
ENCHILADAS MAKE CAFÉ ANNIE A
BENCHMARK FOR QUALITY SOUTHWESTERN
CUISINE.

CAFÉ ANNIE

5860 Westheimer, Houston,
(713) 840-1111, Southwestern, Lunch and dinner Tuesday–Friday,
dinner only Saturday, Reservations suggested, $$$–$$$$

CLIVE'S

517 Louisiana, Houston, (713) 224-4438, Steak, seafood, grilled
specialties, Bar, Extensive Texas wine list, Lunch and dinner Monday-
Saturday, Reservations required, $$$$

CONFEDERATE HOUSE

2925 Weslayan, Houston, (713) 622-1936, American, Bar, Texas wines,
Lunch and dinner Monday–Saturday, Reservations required, $$-$$$

DE VILLE

1300 Lamar in the Four Seasons Hotel,
Houston, (713) 650-1300, Breakfast,
lunch, and dinner Monday–Saturday,
Sunday brunch only, Continental, Bar,
Texas wines, Reservations suggested, $$$

LA RESERVE

4 Riverway in the Omni Hotel, Houston, (713) 871-8177, French, Bar, Texas wines, Lunch and dinner Monday–Saturday, Reservations required, $$$$

LA TOUR D'ARGENT SERVES TOP-SHELF FRENCH CUISINE THAT SHOWCASES SEVERAL EXCELLENT VEAL ENTREES ALONG WITH QUAIL, DUCK, AND OTHER DELECTABLE DISHES.

LA TOUR D'ARGENT

2011 Ella Blvd., Houston, (713) 864-9864, French, Bar, Texas wines, Lunch and dinner Monday–Saturday, Reservations required, $$$$

RAINBOW LODGE

1 Birdsall Street (off Memorial), Houston, (713) 861-8666, Continental, Bar, Texas wines, Lunch and dinner Monday–Friday, dinner only Saturday, Reservations suggested, $$$

ROBERT DEL GRANDE, CHEF AT THE UPSCALE CAFÉ ANNIE, GETS A CHANCE TO SHOW-OFF HIS SKILL WITH DOWN-HOME TEXAS FOOD, SUCH AS XYZ, AT RIO RANCH.

RIO RANCH

9999 Westheimer inside the Hilton Hotel, Houston, (713) 952-5000, Southwestern, Bar, Texas wines, Breakfast, lunch, and dinner daily, Reservations for large or private parties, $$–$$$

RITZ-CARLTON HOTEL

1919 Briar Oaks Lane, Houston, (713) 840-7600, Continental, Bar, Texas wines, Lunch and dinner daily, $$$$

THE STUFFED DOVER SOLE, A 14-OZ. VEAL CHOP, AND TABLESIDE FLAMBÉS MAKE A DRAMATIC IMPRESSION AT THE RIVOLI, AS DOES THE EXTENSIVE WINE LIST.

RIVOLI

5636 Richmond, Houston, (713) 789-1900, Continental, Bar, Texas wines, Lunch and dinner Monday–Friday, dinner only Saturday, Reservations required, $$$–$$$$

ROTISSERIE FOR
BEEF AND BIRD

2200 Wilcrest, Houston, (713) 977-9524, Steak, seafood, grilled specialties, Bar, Extensive Texas wine list, Lunch and dinner Monday-Friday, dinner only Saturday, Reservations required, $$$-$$$$

Old Town Spring

PUFFABELLY'S

100 Main, Old Town Spring, 281-350-3376, Burgers, Sandwiches, Chicken Fried Steak, Beer and wine, House wine is Red River label, Open daily, $$

Chapter 5

WEST TEXAS WINERIES

*V*ast prairies covered with seas of undulating grasses; fractured mountains with mesquite bushes; a sky that goes on forever, interrupted only by a distant thunderhead cloud floating like a jellyfish above with its tentacles of rain dragging across the earth—this is wine country? You bet! This is wine country—West Texas style. In fact, most of the original experimental work done with grapevines in the early 1970s was done in this area. It was here that folks such as Clint McPhearson and Robert Reed, professors at Texas Tech University, and Bobby Smith from La Buena Vida Winery proved that Texas was capable of competing in the wine marketplace.

THE TRAILS

For the sake of our wine trails, West Texas means everything west of the town of Fredericksburg and includes the Panhandle, the High Plains, Trans-Pecos Country, and Big Bend Country. It is a vast area with few people. It is an area where, if you travel down the right road, fences, phone lines, and the arteries of the national power grid disappear. It is also, as some say, going to be the savior of the Texas wine industry. Farmlands around the Lubbock and

◀ **THE LONGER GRAPES REMAIN ON THE VINE, THE SWEETER THEY BECOME. (COURTESY OF THE TEXAS DEPARTMENT OF AGRICULTURE)**

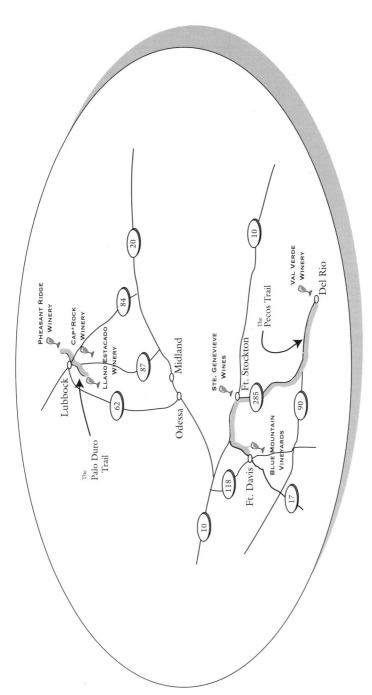

THE WEST TEXAS WINERIES

PALO DURO TRAIL	PECOS TRAIL
❧ Pheasant Ridge Winery	❧ Blue Mountain Vineyard
❧ Llano Estacado Winery	❧ Ste. Genevieve Winery
❧ Cap*Rock Winery	❧ Val Verde Winery

Fort Stockton areas offer some of the best conditions for growing wine-quality grapes. This area is also isolated from Pierce's disease, which is slowly destroying the vineyards of the Hill Country.

The western half of Texas is home to only six wineries and a multitude of vineyards that supply roughly eighty percent of all the grapes and wine in Texas. The large distances between grape-growing areas and the often rugged landscape prompts us to divide these wineries into two trails. The Palo Duo Trail links the wineries around the Lubbock area, and The Pecos Trail connects the wineries near the Pecos River with Val Verde Winery in Del Rio.

Note that some of these wineries, such as Pheasant Ridge near Lubbock, Ste. Genevieve near Fort Stockton, and Blue Mountain Vineyards near Fort Davis do not offer tastings or sales to the public. Tours at some of these wineries are by appointment only and may be restricted to certain times of the year. Call ahead before planning your journey along these trails.

We start our travels in the Lubbock area with a visit to Pheasant Ridge Winery, just north of town.

THE PALO DURO TRAIL

The cloudless, crystal clear sky seems to glimmer as we arrive in Lubbock. Having left the busy metropolitan areas of the great techno-cities of eastern Texas, we step into the vast, fertile fields of the Panhandle. Here atop the escarpment that forms the High Plains, you're tempted to believe that if you squint hard enough, you could see all the way to Canada.

The Palo Duro Trail, named for the magnificent Palo Duro Canyon, just north of the Lubbock area, consists of three wineries: Pheasant Ridge Winery, Llano Estacado Winery, and

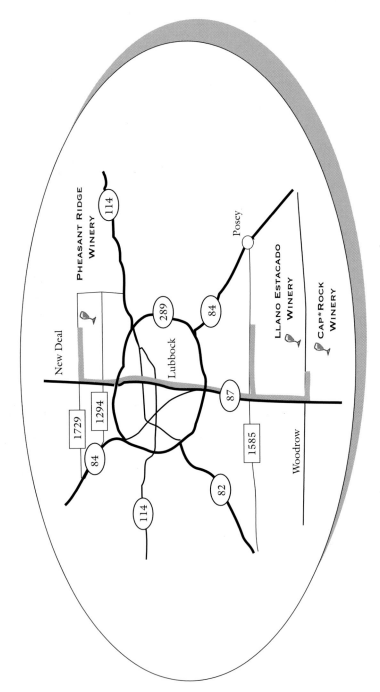

THE PALO DURO TRAIL

114   PHEASANT RIDGE WINERY

New Deal

289

84

Posey

LLANO ESTACADO WINERY

CAP★ROCK WINERY

Lubbock

1729

1294

87

84

1585

Woodrow

114

82

Cap*Rock Winery. Of the three, Pheasant Ridge requires appointments for tours and tastings, and no retail sales are available at the winery itself.

Our first winery on this trail is Pheasant Ridge just north of town, off of SH 87/27. Take the highway to the town of New Deal and right (east) on FM 1729. Pheasant Ridge Winery is approximately three miles from the intersection.

❦Pheasant Ridge Winery

Route 3, Box 191, Lubbock, Texas 79401

Phone: (806) 746-6033; (806) 746-6750

TOURS AND TASTINGS BY APPOINTMENT ONLY

NO RETAIL SALES OR GIFT SHOP

PHEASANT RIDGE

CABERNET SAUVIGNON
TEXAS HIGH PLAINS
1994

PRODUCED & BOTTLED BY PHEASANT RIDGE WINERY, LUBBOCK, TEXAS ALC. 13.2% BY VOL.

When owner Bobby Cox and his wife Jennifer went on their first visit to the California wine country in the early '70s, they returned to Texas disenchanted. The wineries they saw were magnificent complexes of vast vineyards, high-tech equipment and well-tuned marketing organizations. In short, something way beyond their financial horizons. Though they desperately wanted to start a winery in Texas, the California trip made them think they needed that vast scale and technology they saw in California to be able to make a comparable wine.

A trip to France in 1977 for a tour of the wine regions there changed their minds about winemaking. In the most famous French wineries, wine was made in quite primitive conditions, by California standards. It was in France that the Coxes realized that fine wine is not made by stainless steel and glycol coolers— it is made in the vineyard!

Encouraged by what they saw, the Cox family vineyard was planted in 1979. Pheasant Ridge Winery offered its first com-

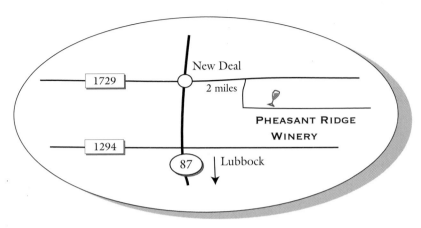

PHEASANT RIDGE WINERY

mercial release in 1984 to wide acclaim. Bobby described Pheasant Ridge as a very small European-style winery, that used the
philosophies and techniques he observed in France. All Pheasant
Ridge wines are made in blended styles, and except for the
Blush, all are aged in French oak.

As the 1990s drew closer for Bobby and Jennifer, the popularity of their wines continued to increase, as did the number of
awards they collected. Based on this early success, the couple incorporated and brought in investors in order to improve the ca-
pabilities of the winery. Pheasant Ridge is now owned by the
Texas Corporation and day-to-day tasks are managed by officers
of the company.

THE WINES

Like numerous other winemakers, Bobby believed that wine
is made in the vineyard first. Quality grapes are necessary for
quality wine, though he does admit that a good winemaker
could make a good wine from lower quality grapes. Much of
the success of these wines can be attributed to the unique conditions enjoyed by the vineyards of the High Plains in Texas.
With well-drained soils at 3,400 feet above sea level, the days
are warm and the nights cool and dry. In this environment,

grapes develop intense flavors in a growing season that runs from April to August.

Under new ownership, the vineyards have been expanded to include Semillion, Chenin Blanc, Merlot, Pinot Noir, and Cabernet Franc. In this perhaps the most French of the Texas wineries, French oak is still heavily used to produce the Bordeaux-style of reds and whites that Pheasant Ridge is famous for. New owner Bill Gipson shares Bobby Cox's preference for French oak and still refers to the wines as "food-style wines."

DIRECTIONS: HEAD SOUTH ON SH 87 THROUGH LUBBOCK AND BEYOND LOOP 289 TO FM 1585. TURN EAST AND YOU ARE JUST A FEW MILES FROM THE NEXT STOP—LLANO ESTACADO WINERY.

ᛜLlano Estacado Winery

P.O. Box 3487, Lubbock, Texas 79452

Phone: (806) 745-2258, Fax: (806) 748-1674

OPEN: 10 A.M.–4 P.M.
MONDAY–SATURDAY; 12–4 P.M.
SUNDAY

TOURS, TASTINGS, RETAIL SALES,
AND GIFT SHOP

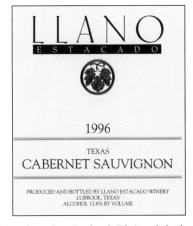

1996

TEXAS

CABERNET SAUVIGNON

PRODUCED AND BOTTLED BY LLANO ESTACADO WINERY
LUBBOCK, TEXAS
ALCOHOL 12.6% BY VOLUME

From its humble beginnings as a casual project on the patio of a Texas horticulturist in the mid '70s, Llano Estacado has grown to be the largest producer of premium wines in the High Plains Appellation. The first wines were released in 1977 under the Staked Plains label, which is still used today for some of Llano's wines. From that initial bottling of 1,300 cases, the winery has grown to produce over 80,000 cases.

The management of Llano Estacado Inc. has undertaken an effort to increase their share of the American wine market, as

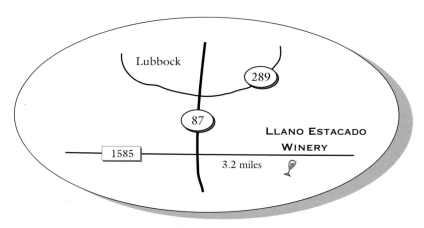

LLANO ESTACADO WINERY

well as to raise the level of quality of their wines. As part of that effort, the company hired veteran California winemaker Greg Bruni in 1993. Mr. Bruni's winemaking experience dates back to 1977 when he graduated from the University of California-Davis. He also comes from a family with three generations of winemaking experience. Working for a variety of successful wineries in California, Greg was rewarded for his efforts with an impressive array of medals and honors.

Walter Haimman, president of Llano Estacado Winery, said "Greg brings an entirely new and higher level of experience to the Texas wine industry and certainly to Llano Estacado." Mr. Haimman feels that Llano Estacado could not undertake current efforts to increase the winery's visibility and quality of its products without Greg on board.

The quality of Llano Estacado wines is confirmed by the innumerable awards it has collected recently. Highly respected in America, these wines enjoy national as well as international distribution throughout Europe. Interestingly, the popularity of these wines has spilled over into the political arena as well. Llano Estacado wines were served by President Reagan in the White House, at the Houston Economic Summit, and at the Bush-Gorbachev Summit. Queen Elizabeth was served Llano Estacado wine during her visit to the United States.

VIEW OF LLANO ESTACADO WINERY FROM THE ROADWAY.

THE WINES

For a grape, Llano Estacado Winery must seem like a paradise. The winery has great growing conditions in the High Plains viticulture area with warm days and cool nights, plenty of water, and some of the best equipment to squeeze out the juices without bruising and damaging the fruit.

Greg Bruni shares winemaker Dean Valentine's belief that the High Plains area of Texas has great potential for world-class grape production—they just have to perfect their techniques. What works in California or Europe may not be the best practice in the High Plains. Part of the experimentation at Llano includes the use of mechanical harvesters and the purchase of low-pressure bladder presses to slowly extract the juice without damaging the fruit and releasing unwanted chemical compounds into the juice.

Llano markets a variety of wines under the Llano Estacado label including Chardonnay, Sauvignon Blanc, Merlot, and Cabernet Sauvignon. A selection of lower-priced table wines is sold under the Staked Plains label.

DIRECTIONS: AFTER ENJOYING YOUR STAY WITH LLANO ESTACADO, HEAD BACK TO SH 87 AND CONTINUE SOUTH TO WOODROW ROAD AND TURN EASTWARD TO THE MAGNIFICENT CAP*ROCK WINERY.

♣Cap*Rock Winery

Route 6, Box 713K, Lubbock, Texas 79423
Phone: (806) 863-2704, Fax: (806) 863-2712

> OPEN: 10 A.M.–5 P.M.
> MONDAY–SATURDAY; 12–5 P.M.
> SUNDAY
>
> TOURS, TASTINGS, RETAIL SALES,
> AND GIFT SHOP

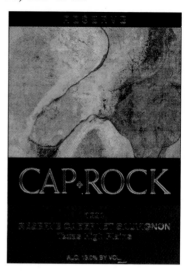

Cap*Rock is possibly the most attractive of all the existing Texas wineries, an architectural jewel set in the High Plains. Originally built for Teysha Wine Cellars, this $5 million facility was purchased by the Plains Capital Corporation in 1990. As a magnificent example of Southwestern architecture, the well-appointed visitors center/tasting room beckons visitors in to relax, tour the facilities, and sample some exceptional wines.

THE MAGNIFICENT ARCHITECTURE OF CAP*ROCK WINERY.

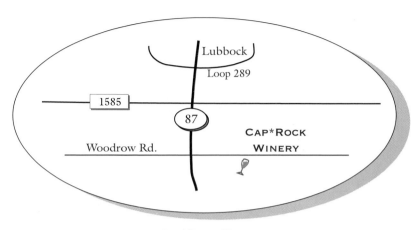

CAP*ROCK WINERY

The winery's name is derived from the geological formation it sits on, which extends from the High Plains up into the northern part of the Texas Panhandle. In geological terms, a caprock is an impenetrable layer of sediment set down during a single geological period. The Cap*Rock label is a creative depiction of this geological formation. The subtle technique of the minimalist design allows for varied interpretation of the Cap*Rock label. Some see a geological formation, while others see an abstract painting, and the romantics among us, see an embrace.

Ninety-eight of the 119 acres at this facility are cultivated as vineyards, and yet, you will not find the Estate Bottled designation on any of the labels shown here. Even with this amount of vines planted, additional grapes must be purchased from area growers to support this modern facility, capable of storing 139,000 gallons of wine. Of course without a strong commitment to quality and a vintner with a firm hand on the winemaking process, even the most modern of wineries would not produce premium quality wines. For this reason the owners hired Kim McPhearson as Cap*Rock's winemaker.

Kim's internship in the Napa Valley wine industry is enhanced by years of expertise in the Texas wine industry and by association with several successful wineries. His efforts in Texas over the years have produced wines that have won more than 300 medals

THE WELL-APPOINTED TASTING ROOM AT CAP*ROCK WINERY.

at tasting events throughout the United States. By using a combination of stainless-steel tanks with American and French oak barrels, Kim keeps fermentation lots small to allow the wine to develop to its full potential.

THE WINES

Cap*Rock produces eleven different wines divided into four price groups, called tiers:

Tier I: Sparkling Brut
            Reserve Cabernet Sauvignon

Tier II: Chardonnay
            Cabernet Sauvignon
            Muscat Canelli
            Merlot

Tier III: Cabernet Royale
            Diamond Royale
            Garnet Royale
            Topaz Royale

Tier IV: Blush

Tier I wines are Cap*Rock's premium labels. The Sparkling Brut is a blend of Chardonnay and Pinot Noir, produced in the classic *Methode Champenoise* of France. The Cabernet Sauvignon is a full-bodied wine with rich color and oak-aged highlights. The winemaker feels that this wine will continue to age well in the bottle for at least five years.

Tier II wines have been briefly aged in oak to enhance the character of the grape with just a hint of the oak flavor present. These wines have been crafted by the winemaker as ready-to-drink wines. Tier III and Tier IV wines represent Cap*Rock's table wine selection. These highly drinkable wines represent some of the most ambitious blending done by Kim McPhearson. The Garnet Royale is a blend of Cabernet Sauvignon, Cabernet Franc, and Pinot Noir that results in a dry, soft wine. The Topaz Royale is a blend of Chenin Blanc, Johannesberg Reisling, and Muscat Canelli, resulting in a fruity, sweeter wine.

The popularity of Cap*Rock's award-winning wines has forced management to begin plans to expand the winery and the vineyard. A new barrel room for red wines is planned to satisfy the struggle for space in the existing Red Room. Seems that the barrels have to compete for space with the people who want the room for special events such as parties and private dinners. The beauti-

AN INSPIRING DISPLAY OF WINES.

A BARREL
"NURSERY" FOR
MATURING
WINES.

ful decor of this high-ceiling, heavily wood-paneled room has made it popular; the room is often booked three times a week.

The vineyard will also be expanded with an experimental planting for new varietals.

ALONG THE TRAIL

The High Plains of Texas are filled with great western wilderness, pioneer spirit, and numerous historical sites. Near Canyon, just south of Amarillo, off IH 27 is perhaps the largest attraction in this area—Palo Duro Canyon. Named for the hardwoods that grow here, the Palo Duro Canyon State Park covers more than 15,000 acres of this geological area. This canyon was carved out of the plateau by a branch of the Red River, exposing rock formations and beautiful vistas, that are now accessible via paved roads.

The musical drama *Texas* draws international crowds annually to this region. Performed against the rugged canyon wall, this musical lets the audience experience the pioneer story in song and dance. The state park is open year round with a small admission charge per vehicle. The musical is performed in the summer months, nightly except Sunday. Tickets are under $15 per person, and reservations are necessary. Call (806) 655-2181 for information and reservations. And remember—dress warm, the evenings can get a bit cool in these parts.

The town of Plainview lies between Canyon and Lubbock and offers antique shopping in the historical downtown district. The Llano Estacado Museum exhibits pioneer life collections and archeological-site remains of prehistoric mammoths and armadillos that grew up to six feet long! A small admission fee is requested.

The Lubbock area offers a unique combination of history and entertainment. The Buddy Holly Statue and the Walk of Fame feature numerous contributions by many West Texas natives, with of course, a special salute to Mr. Holly. The historic district offers a nightlife of fine restaurants and a wide selection of live music guaranteed to provide a good time for all. Scenic drives south of this area are a yearly favorite for many travelers to this area. Pack a picnic basket and take in the breathtaking views of the canyons in the Texas High Plains.

THE PECOS TRAIL

The Pecos River Valley is an almost uninhabited river basin. In the distance loom the rugged Davis Mountains, announcing a remote land that once boasted being home to desperadoes who fled to the "bad lands." Fortunately, you won't have to go quite that far into the area—unless, of course, you like backcountry expeditions. The Pecos Trail, named for the Pecos River with its "West of the Pecos" history, begins approximately 200 miles south and east of Lubbock, in the foothills of the Davis Mountains.

The longest wine trail in the state, at approximately 300 miles end to end, this trail is best approached as a long weekend trip, allowing for an overnight stay along the way. From the Davis Mountains, which serve as home to Blue Mountain Winery, Ste. Genevieve Winery, and the McDonald Observatory, you will swoop down along SH 90 and close in on the Rio Grande River as you near Del Rio to visit Texas' oldest operating winery, Val Verde Winery. You will pass through mountain towns like Balmorhea, Fort Davis, and Alpine, and see dramatic views of some of the highest peaks in Texas, such as Timber Mountain, Mt. Livermore, and Cathedral Mountain. Take plenty of film with you on this trip.

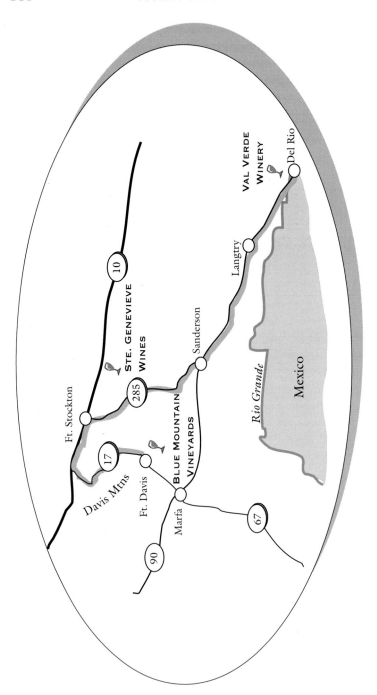

THE PECOS TRAIL WINERIES

Leaving Fort Stockton, you will notice the land continues to rise before you as you travel west along SH 10 to SH 17 and south for approximately forty miles to the town of Fort Davis, home of Blue Mountain Vineyards.

❧Blue Mountain Vineyards

HCR 74, Box 7, Fort Davis, Texas 79734
Phone: (915) 426-3763, Fax: (915) 426-3763

TOURS AND TASTINGS BY
APPOINTMENT

NO RETAIL SALES OR
GIFT SHOP

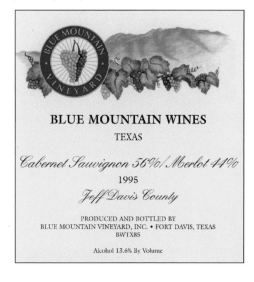

BLUE MOUNTAIN WINES

TEXAS

Cabernet Sauvignon 56% / Merlot 44%

1995

Jeff Davis County

PRODUCED AND BOTTLED BY
BLUE MOUNTAIN VINEYARD, INC. • FORT DAVIS, TEXAS
BWTX85

Alcohol 13.6% By Volume

Life in the mountains is different somehow. Brilliant sun-filled days warm the mountainsides, allowing plants and animals to flourish in this steeply sloped world. Nightfall brings cool, crisp evening and a night sky packed with stars. Rainfall, temperatures, and the tempo of life itself are all controlled by the mountains. Patience, hailed as a virtue by the civilized world, is a necessity for living and thriving in this mountain environment. Patrick Johnson, winemaker at Blue Mountain Vineyards, understands the importance of such patience, as does owner Nell Weisbach.

Set at 5,300 feet above sea level in the dramatic beauty of the Davis Mountains, Blue Mountain Vineyards has been producing red and white grapes of superior quality for over a decade for vintners around the state. Patrick, who was educated at University of California at Davis and apprenticed at one of the largest wineries in California, patiently waited for Nell to have the winery bonded to produce wines. In the interim, he studied the

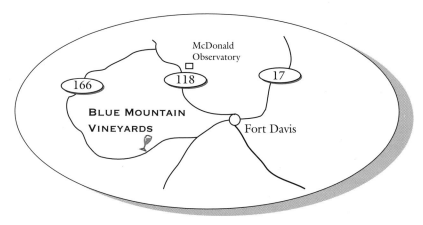

BLUE MOUNTAIN VINEYARDS

unique characteristics of the Fort Davis area and applied his winemaking skills to nurturing his grapes to produce great wines. Bonded in 1994, Blue Mountain Vineyards has been producing award-wining wines ever since.

The scenic vineyard snuggled into the side of Blue Mountain contains fifty-five acres of Cabernet Sauvignon, Merlot, Sauvignon Blanc, and Chenin Blanc. Patrick uses these grapes exclusively to produce Cabernet Sauvignon, a Cabernet Sauvignon/Merlot blend, made in the Bordeaux style, a Sauvignon Blanc, and a white table wine made from Chenin Blanc and Sauvignon Blanc. He uses all his own grapes and does not bring grapes in from other vineyards in order to produce wines that can be classified as Estate Bottled. The word "estate" on a wine label signifies that the wine was made at the winery from grapes grown at the winery's vineyard.

When you taste Blue Mountain Vineyards' wines, however, you will notice that "estate" doesn't appear on any of the bottles. Here's where that patience thing comes into play again. Another requirement of the estate label is that the winery must be located in a viticultural appellation—that is, an area recognized for specific growing conditions that give the wines produced there a unique quality. When we spoke with Patrick, the appellation title was about to be granted after more than two years of work. Yes, patience truly is a virtue!

THE WINES

During our conversation, Patrick used a term to describe himself that we have not often heard. He referred to himself as a winegrower, instead of a winemaker. As he explains it, "Wine is made in the field. You can't have a quality wine without first having quality grapes." At an elevation of 5,300 feet, Blue Mountain Vineyards is blessed with cool nights even in the months of July and August, which allow the grapes to ripen slowly on the vine. By stretching out the crucial ripening phase to seven or eight weeks, the vinter allows the vines time to work their magic on the grapes to metabolize a multitude of components into the fruit.

As a result, the wines produced by Blue Mountain Vineyards are fruity, full-mouthed wines of a remarkable rich color. Patrick also has the advantage of being able to crush the grapes within hours of being picked, something he feels adds greatly to the final flavor of the wine. Using oak sparingly, he tries to age his reds for at least a year. Like many vinters, Patrick prefers to produce red wines that are a blend of French and American oak aging, ". . . a blending of the two is really nice, in my opinion."

With around 1,000 cases a year, Blue Mountain Vineyards wines are not available all across Texas. Outside of the winery, you can find them in the Midland/Odessa, El Paso, and Dallas areas. Patrick is working on expanding the list of locations, but as with everything else, it takes time. It's good he is a patient man!

DIRECTIONS: FROM BLUE MOUNTAIN VINEYARDS DOUBLE BACK ALONG SH 17 TO SH 10 TO RETURN TO FORT STOCKTON TO VISIT STE. GENEVIEVE WINERY. IF YOU WOULD LIKE A MORE SCENIC ROUTE, TAKE SH 118 SOUTH TO SH 67 AND TURN LEFT (NORTHEAST) FOR A SIXTY-SEVEN MILE TRIP THROUGH THE GLASS MOUNTAINS.

&Ste. Genevieve Winery (Cordier Estates)

P.O. Box 697, Fort Stockton, Texas 79735

Phone: (915) 395-2417, Fax: (915) 395-2431

Ste. Genevieve Winery is located just outside of Ft. Stockton on land owned by the University of Texas and leased to Cordier Estates Winery. Out here, everything is BIG. The vineyard covers more than 1,000 acres, making it the largest in Texas. Matching the scale of the vineyard is the winery's fermenting capacity at 1.2 million gallons! Yes, this is big country. The vines stretch out into the shadow of the Skyscraper Mesa that dominates the visual horizon here. The word "mesa" is taken from the Spanish word for table, which aptly describes these stark monolithics set against the vast West Texas sky.

The vineyard is unique in many ways. It is supplied with an ample supply of water from an underground aquifer and uses drip irrigation to conserve water usage in this arid area. The size of the available land also allows large spacing between vines and between vine rows, making the use of mechanical harvesters quite easy. Though somewhat lower in altitude than the Lubbock area wineries, Ste. Genevieve enjoys similar soil conditions and temperature ranges to promote juicy, healthy fruit. The Escondido Valley in which the vineyard is located is surrounded by expanses of desert, effectively isolating the vineyard from other horticultural areas. The result is a virtually pest-free environment—a big plus considering recent outbreaks of Pierce's disease around the state.

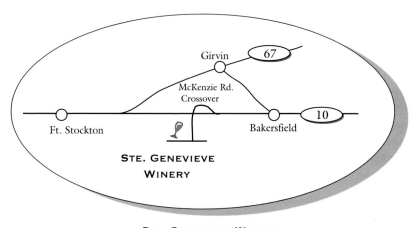

STE. GENEVIEVE WINERY

THE WINES

The name Ste. Genevieve was taken from Genevieve, the patron saint of Paris, who is credited with saving the city and its vineyards by turning away Attila the Hun's troops. With such a rich tradition and a owner like Domaines Cordier—the largest vineyard owner in France—it's not surprising to see a French influence in the winemaking.

Don Brady, often referred to as the most-awarded winemaker in Texas, oversees the winemaking process of what is the largest winery in Texas. The Ste. Genevieve label includes more than a dozen wines represented by three distinct wine groupings: The Proprietor's Reserve, the Ste. Genevieve Varietals, and the Ste. Genevieve Classics. Produced from grapes grown in the Escondido viticultural area, these wines appeal to all tastes and pocketbooks, and are readily available in most grocery stores in Texas. The managing company constantly upgrades the facilities to produce a wider range of products. The grapes now grown in the vineyard include Cabernet Franc, Merlot, Barbera, Zinfandel, Pinot Noir, Cabernet Sauvignon, Ruby Cabernet, Chenin Blanc, Chardonnay, Sauvignon Blanc, Muscat, and French Columbard.

The Proprietor's Reserve label offers limited releases of hand-crafted Chardonnay and Cabernet Sauvignon. The estate-bottled Chardonnay is fermented in both French and American oak to give it a crisp, fruity flavor with a hint of vanilla and oak. It has been crafted for immediate consumption. The Cabernet Sauvignon, however, while perfectly drinkable at the time of bottling, will also age well in the bottle for a number of years.

The lower-priced Ste. Genevieve Varietals represent a selection of award-winning varietals at a more affordable price. Included in this category are: Texas Cabernet Sauvignon, Texas Chenin Blanc, American White Zinfandel, Texas Merlot, Texas Classic Red, Texas Chardonnay, and Texas Sauvignon Blanc. This popular group of wines is widely available in grocery and liquor stores across the state.

Finally, the Texas Classics represent Ste. Genevieve's table wines: Texas First Blush, Texas Blush, Texas White, and Texas Red. A spokesperson at Ste. Genevieve told us the winery will soon release a new mid-range premium group of wines (750 ml size) and a new Zinfandel (750 ml size).

A brief note on touring this winery. Ste. Genevieve does not host tours and tastings. Tours are available, however, through the Fort Stockton Chamber of Commerce, which holds vineyard and winery tours and tastings on Wednesday and Saturday mornings. You can contact the Fort Stockton Chamber of Commerce at 915-395-2417. Wines are also available for sale at the end of the tour. Remember though, don't just show up at the winery. You won't be admitted unless you are part of the Chamber of Commerce tour group.

DIRECTIONS: FROM STE. GENEVIEVE IT IS APPROXIMATELY A 200 MILE JOURNEY TO DEL RIO TO VISIT VAL VERDE WINERY. TRAVEL SOUTH ON SH 285 TO THE TOWN OF SANDERSON. TURN SOUTH ONTO SH 90 AND CONTINUE ON TO DEL RIO, PASSING OVER THE AMISTAD RESERVOIR. IF YOU PLAN TO DRIVE THIS LEG OF THE TRAIL, GIVE YOURSELF PLENTY OF TIME.

⚜Val Verde Winery

100 Qualia Drive, Del Rio, Texas 78840

Phone: (830) 775-9714

OPEN : 9 A.M.–5 P.M.
MONDAY–SATURDAY

TOURS, TASTINGS, RETAIL SALES,
AND GIFT SHOP

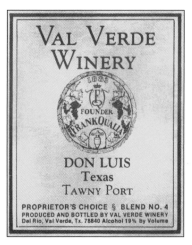

Tucked into this hot, dry corner of South Texas you will find an oasis called Del Rio, nicknamed Queen of the Rio Grande. Del Rio sits atop the cool, refreshing waters of the San Felipe Springs, which pours out over 90 million gallons of crystal clear water daily. When Frank Qualia purchased his land in Del Rio in 1882 to become a farmer, a number of Lenoir grapevines were already growing. The abundance of water and the obvious health of the grapevines prompted Frank to start his vineyard more than 100 years ago.

Val Verde Winery is the oldest in Texas, and the only one to survive the Prohibition. Unlike most other winemakers, the Qualia family tended to their vineyard during the Prohibition and used the grapes to produce jellies, sacramental wines, and also shipped grapes to cities such as Houston and Galveston for fruit consumption. Following the repeal of Prohibition, second-generation winemaker Louis Qualia planned the resumption of commercial winemaking and introduced the Herbemont grape to the vineyard for diversification and increased production.

Tom Qualia, third-generation winemaker, assumed care of the winery in 1973. Although he originally planned to become a rancher, his love of winemaking and its place in family tradition made him totally dedicated to what his family had accomplished.

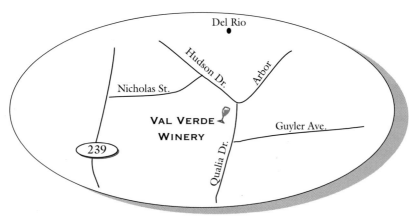

VAL VERDE WINERY

After a concentrated effort to modernize and improve the facilities during the 1970s and 1980s, Val Verde still concentrates on the production of Lenoir and Herbemont grapes, which are well-suited to the environment. Tom replaced all but two of his father's original 2,350-gallon concrete tanks with new stainless-steel tanks. He continues his father's commitment to making "a few good bottles of wine."

THE WINES

Val Verde Winery produces an impressive selection of wines that includes Sauvignon Blanc, Muscat Canelli, Ruby Cabernet, Lenoir, and a newcomer—Ehrenfelser, a fruity white with a German heritage. Last, but perhaps the most well-known and most-awarded Val Verde wine is their exceptional Tawny Port Don Luis, produced in honor of Tom's father.

Val Verde produces approximately 3,000 cases of wine annually, and the majority of its sales is at the winery itself. A limited selection of its wine can be found around the state, particularly in the larger cities such as Austin, Houston, and Dallas/Ft. Worth.

ALONG THE TRAIL

The sun doesn't just set in this part of Texas, it crashes into the desert around you, as the evening sky goes from pale rose to blood red before being swallowed in inky blackness. The Pecos Trail travels through some of the most remote areas of Texas, where tumbleweed and sagebrush are king. On the west end of the trail, the McDonald Observatory sits majestically atop the Davis Mountains, while the lush beauty of the Amistad Reservior waits for you on the east end of the trail.

This is, of course, a trail for wine lovers, but it is also much more. It is a trail for reflection and contemplation. It is a journey that may show travelers something of themselves in addition to Texas wines. The wide-open spaces and the star-filled evenings are perfect for thinking about the past and considering the potential of the future. As the sun sinks behind the mountains, there is a moment, just before the stars invade the night, when time seems to stand still and everything is possible.

Just south of Fort Davis are the towns of Marfa and Alpine. Though only about twenty-six miles apart, these towns seem to be separated by half a century in time. Marfa is a town that has changed little over the years, and has become popular with artists and sculptors. By contrast, Alpine, which is on the route for tourists heading down to the Big Bend National Park, is a modern-day fast-food wonderland.

Leaving these towns behind, you pass Marathon on SH 90 and leave the last of the mountain ranges behind you, as you enter Hell's Half Acre—not exactly a popular resort acre. Keep plenty to drink on hand, gas up the car, and cruise for the Pecos River. The town of Langtry, which lies ahead of you, was home to Judge Roy Bean, known as the "Law West of the Pecos." Where the Pecos joins the Rio Grande River, the land changes from parched desert to lush greenery as you enter the Amistad National Recreation Area. The sleepy town of Del Rio lies just beyond the reservoir.

BED AND BREAKFAST
ALONG THE PALO DURO TRAIL

Canyon

COUNTRY HOME BED AND BREAKFAST AND MOM'S PLACE

Host: Tammy Money-Brooks, Rt. 1, Box 447, Canyon 79015,
(800) 664-7636 or (806) 655-7636, 4 rooms, 3½ baths, 1 guest house,
full breakfast, $–$$$, no pets, no smoking, MC, V, AE, D

THE HUDSPETH HOUSE

Hosts: Mark and Mary Clark, 1905 4th Ave., Canyon 79015,
(800) 655-9809, (806) 655-9800, fax (806) 655-7457,
8 guest rooms, 8 baths, full breakfast, $–$$$, MC, V, AE, D

Lubbock

WOODROW HOUSE

Hosts: Dawn and David Fleming, 2629 19th St., Lubbock 79410, (806)
793-3330, fax (806) 793-7676, 7 guest rooms, 7 private baths, breakfast
buffet, $$, children welcome, no pets, no smoking, MC, V, AE

VIRGINIA'S BED AND BREAKFAST

Host: Virginia Baker, 310 Breckenridge, Albany 76430, (915) 762-2013, 3 guest rooms, 3 baths, 1 suite, 1 guest house, country or continental breakfast, $$, no pets, smoking, no alcohol, no cr

RESTAURANTS
ALONG THE PALO DURO TRAIL

Canyon

COPE'S CONEY ISLAND

2201 Fourth Ave., Canyon, (806) 655-1184, Homestyle fried chicken, fried fish, club steak, homemade pies, Breakfast, lunch, and dinner Monday-Saturday, $

Lubbock

COUNTY LINE

FM 2641 west of IH-27 N., Lubbock, (806) 763-6001, Barbecue, Bar, Texas wines, Dinner daily, $-$$

STUBB'S BAR-B-Q

620 Nineteenth St., Lubbock, (806) 747-4777, Barbecue, Bar, Texas wines, Lunch and dinner daily, $

BED AND BREAKFASTS
ALONG THE PECOS TRAIL

Alpine

HOLLAND HOTEL

Host: Carla McFarland, 209 W. Holland Ave., Alpine 79830, (915) 837-3844 or (800) 535-8040, 10 guest rooms, 10 baths, penthouse, continental plus breakfast OYO, children welcome, pets okay by prior arrangement, smoking in two guest rooms, $–$$, MC, V, AE

THE CORNER HOUSE

Host: Jim Glendinning, 801 East Ave. E., Alpine 79830, (800) 585-7795 or (915) 837-7161, fax (915) 837-3638, 6 guest rooms, 4 private baths, 1 shared bath, country or continental breakfast, $, smoking only on porch, MC, V, AE, D

THE WHITE HOUSE INN

Host: Anita Bradney, 2003 Fort Davis Hwy., Alpine 79830, (888) 774-7171 or (915) 837-1401, fax (915) 837-2197, 6 guest rooms, 6 baths, 1 guest house, gourmet breakfast, $$, children over 12 welcome, no pets, no smoking, MC, V, D

Del Rio

THE 1890 HOUSE

Hosts: Alberto and Laura Galvan, 609 Griner Street, Del Rio 78840, (800) 282-1360 or (210) 775-8061, fax (210) 775-4667, 3 rooms, 1 suite, gourmet breakfast, $$–$$$$, no pets, MC, V

Fort Davis

NEILL MUSEUM B&B

Host: Shirley Neill Vickers, P.O. Box 1034, Fort Davis 79734, (915) 426-3838 or (915) 426-3969, 2 rooms, 2 baths, continental breakfast OYO, $–$$$, no children, pets, or smoking, no cr

THE VERANDA COUNTRY INN

Hosts: Kathie and Paul Woods, 210 Court Avenue, Fort Davis 79734, (888) 383-2847, 3 guest rooms, 5 suites, 1 guest house, private baths, full breakfast, $–$$$$, no pets, no smoking, MC, V, D

Marathon

CAPTAIN SHEPARD'S INN

Co-managers: Bill and Laurie Stevens, P.O. Box 46, Marathon 79842, (800) 884-4243, fax (915) 386-4510, 5 guest rooms, 6 baths, full breakfast, $$$, children welcome, but no pets, smoking in one sitting room, all cr

RESTAURANTS ALONG
THE PECOS TRAIL

Alpine

CORNER HOUSE CAFÉ

801 E. Ave. E, Alpine, (915) 837-7161, Breakfast and lunch Tuesday–Saturday, $

LITTLE MEXICO CAFÉ

204 W. Murphy Ave., Alpine, (915) 837-2855, Mexican, Beer, Lunch and dinner Monday–Saturday, $

PONDEROSA INN RESTAURANT

East Hwy. 90, Alpine, (915) 837-3321, American, Breakfast, lunch, and dinner daily, $

Del Rio

CRIPPLE CREEK SALOON

US 90 about one mile west of the "Y" with US 277/377, Del Rio, (830) 775-0153, Steak and seafood, Bar, Texas wines, Dinner Monday–Saturday, $$

MEMO'S

804 E. Losoya, Del Rio, (830) 775-8104, American and Tex-Mex, Bar, Lunch and dinner Monday–Saturday, Dinner only Sunday, $-$$

Fort Davis

BLACK BEAR RESTAURANT AT THE INDIAN LODGE

Davis Mountains State Park, 4 miles northwest of Fort Davis via SH-118, Fort Davis, (915) 426-3254, American, Open daily, $

THE DRUGSTORE RESTAURANT

At the Old Texas Inn, Fort Davis, (915) 426-3118, American and Tex-Mex, Soda Fountain fare such as floats, malts, sundaes, and phosphates, Breakfast and lunch, closed Wednesday, $

HIGHWAY 118 CAFÉ

Hwy. 118 south of Fort Davis, (915) 426-3934, American and Tex-Mex, Open 6:30 A.M.–8:30 P.M. Tuesday–Sunday, closed 2:30 P.M.–5:30 P.M., $

HOTEL LIMPIA DINING ROOM

Main Street at the Town Square, Fort Davis, (915) 426-3241, American, Bar, including Texas wines, in The Bandana Room bar ($3 membership fee for non-hotel guests required by state law in this "dry" county), Dinner daily, Breakfast and lunch Saturday–Sunday, $–$$

Marathon

GLASS MOUNTAIN BAR AND GRILL

Inside the Gage Hotel, Marathon, (915) 386-4205, Breakfast, lunch, and dinner daily, Southwestern, Bar, Texas wines, $–$$

Chapter 6

FESTIVALS AND
SPECIAL EVENTS

*W*hen Texans like something, they celebrate it in a big way, and their pride in Texas wines is no exception. Festivals and special events sponsored by wineries and organizations are held around the state throughout the year. As you plan your tours along the Texas wine trails, keep these events in mind. Every festival brings out the best of the food, music, and wine of each sponsoring locale. Many wine-related festivals are now annual events that are held about the same time each year, which makes it convenient to plan yearly trips. Individual winery events may change each year, so it is best to contact the wineries ahead of time. Some of the wineries will even place your name on their mailing list of upcoming events and new wine releases.

Listed below are the major wine-related festivals in Texas that are open to the public during the spring, summer, and fall seasons. It is worth noting that while wine events occur throughout the year, the months of April and October are particularly busy times for festivals, and festival goers can enjoy some of the most colorful scenes in Texas during these months. April is bluebonnet time, when the roadsides are awash in violet blues and the orange hues of the Indian paintbrush blossoms. In October, fall colors sneak into Texas where you'd least expect them. The

◀ A VARIETAL WINE MUST CONTAIN 75% BY VOLUME OF THE GRAPE MENTIONED ON THE LABEL. (COURTESY OF THE TEXAS DEPARTMENT OF AGRICULTURE)

days are sunny and comfortable and the evenings crisp and clear—perfect weather for attending the festivals.

Spring Events

Denison Arts and Wine Festival

Old Katy Depot in Denison, Texas
(817) 424-0570
March; call for dates

One of the newest wine festivals in Texas, this well-organized event drew large enthusiatic crowds at its premier. It is a celebration of Texas wine and the visual and musical arts of local artists around Denison. Bring the family to enjoy the live entertainment and food from local Denison restaurants.

Lubbock Cork and Fork Affair

Lubbock, Texas
(806) 742-3077
March; call for dates

Held in the Lubbock Memorial Civic Center, the Cork and Fork Affair is a wondrous mix of food and wine, with more than 30 restaurants and over a dozen Texas wineries offerings tastings of their products. For the price of the entry ticket (around $25), you get to eat and drink as much as you want. Besides the good food and wine, guests may enjoy live music and meet people from restaurants and wineries across the state. Always a sell-out, be sure to book ahead each year. Tickets are available at the door or from the Lubbock Chamber of Commerce.

Texas Hill Country Wine and Food Festival

Four Seasons Hotel, Austin
(512) 329-0770
April; call for dates

This festival is a must for adults who love sampling good wine and food in one of America's most elegant and charming hotels. The Four Seasons Hotel is the backdrop for this four-day event that includes wine-tasting sessions of both Texas and California wines, seminars and tastings of the creations of some of this country's finest chefs, and a fabulous dinner and dance. A particular favorite event of this festival is the Wine-maker's Luncheon in which attendees select from one of five great Austin restaurants to break bread with winemakers. Each day is packed full of events and all are priced separately, so call for details.

New Vintage Festival

Grapevine, Texas
(800) 457-6338
April; call for dates

The newest releases of Texas wines are celebrated during this three-day event. The festival includes the traditional Blessing of the Vines ceremony, seminars of winemaking and food and wine pairings, and the popular Taste and Toast of Texas during which the public taste Texas wines in downtown Grapevine.

Texas Hill Country Wildflowers and Wine Trail

Participating Wineries in the Hill Country
(817) 424-0570
April; call for dates

It doesn't get any better than this—the beauty of wildflowers in the Hill Country and the enjoyment of delicious local wines. All the wineries along the Enchanted and Highland Wine Trails participate in this extremely popular event. The event features tours, tastings, food, music, and fun for all. For details of activities, contact the wineries along the Enchanted and Highland Wine Trails.

Texas Wine and Brew Festival

San Angelo, Texas
(915) 653-6793
April; call for dates

This weekend festival kicks off on Friday with a Gourmet Dinner, a six-course meal presented each year by a well-known Texas chef. Reservations are required and seating is limited, so be sure to call ahead. On Saturday morning, cooking classes are followed by the Wine, Brew and Food Tasting, featuring Texas wineries, microbreweries and more than a dozen of San Angelo's restaurants and caterers. Live music is also available. All events are priced separate, so call ahead for information.

Dallas Morning News Wine Awards

Fairmont Hotel
(214) 319-7000
May; call for dates

The public is invited to sample the wines from the wineries that participated in the Dallas Morning News Wine Competition which is held in March. Wineries from across the state are pouring their wines.

SUMMER EVENTS

Annual Kerrville Folk Festival

Kerrville, Texas
(800) 435-8429
May; call for dates

Enjoy great Texas music, food, and wine. Prices vary by events and weekends, so call for information.

Rockport Festival of Wines

Rockport, Texas

(512) 729-1271

June; call for dates

The picturesque town of Rockport on the Texas Gulf Coast is host to one of the most delightful wine festivals in the state. The Rockport Festival of Wines is a summer traveler's delight, offering generous tastings of Texas' finest wines and food from popular local restaurants. Plan on staying the weekend in this coastal resort town to enjoy the sights and sounds Rockport has to offer.

Pecos County Harvest Fest

Rooney Park, Ft. Stockton, Texas

(915) 336-2541

August; call for dates

This is a great festival and a great way to experience the hospitality of West Texas. This high energy festival includes a three-mile run, a bike tour to Ste. Genevieve Winery (and a winery tour), a huge car show, food and craft booths, and live music. At noon the Wine Emporium opens up featuring wines from numerous Texas wineries.

Annual Kerrville Wine and Music Festival

Kerrville, Texas

(800) 435-8429

Labor Day Weekend

This event features the best and newest works from Texas winemakers and more than two dozen Texas songwriters. Outdoor theaters host afternoon and evening concerts and food and wine stands are available throughout the festival. Prices vary and three-day passes are available. Bring lawn chairs and wear rugged clothing (jeans, boots, sun hats) for this primitive but beautiful setting.

FALL EVENTS

Grapefest

Grapevine, Texas

(800) 457-6338

September; call for dates

Grapefest is undoubtedly the biggest wine festival in Texas, with attendance at well over 100,000 folks during this three-day event. Downtown Grapevine is transformed into a huge carnival setting with rides for the kids, face painting, food, live music, and of course Texas wines. The People's Choice, an event in which the public gets to vote on the best wines, is a favorite part of this festival.

Annual Harvest Festival

Grapevine, Texas

(817) 424-0570

September; call for dates

Sponsored by the Texas Wine and Grape Growers Association, this festival brings together professionals from all facets of the Texas wine industry and provides opportunities to learn about grape growing and winemaking in the Lone Star state.

Uncorking Texas Wines Tasting

(817) 424-0570

This popular public food and wine event is usually held in conjunction with the Annual Harvest Festival. Call for additional information.

Fredericksburg Food and Wine Festival

Fredericksburg, Texas

(830) 997-7467

October; call for dates

Each year this determined community of 7,500 puts together an impressive collection of Texas wines, food, and entertainment. The admission price of $12 for adults includes five wine tastings and a souvenir wine glass. Inside the festival grounds are two large pavilions, a bandstand, picnic tables, and just a whole lot of fun. One pavilion houses more than a dozen Texas wineries offering samples of the best vintages, while the other pavilion contains dozens of exhibitors of Texas crafts and food. As you stroll between pavilions, enjoy the sounds of the Hill Country's performers playing blues, jazz, ethnic, and country tunes.

Festival attractions also include a grape stomp and the infamous Great Grape Toss, with an auction to top all auctions. The first evening of the festival a dinner with some of the vintners attending is held at one of the local restaurants and features Texas wines. The second day of the festival features a gourmet luncheon. Both of these special events are part of the festival patron program and include general admission to the festival. Tickets are usually available on a limited basis and sold in advance only.

Kristkindl Markt

Fredericksburg, Texas
(830) 997-8515
December weekend; call for dates

Soft carols, fresh-cut pine trees and booths stuffed full of Christmas ideas and gifts await shoppers attending this Christmas shopping festival each December. Held in downtown Fredericksburg's Martplatz, this event is an updated version of the seventeenth-century German Christmas market. Shoppers will be able to hear German music and other entertainment, enjoy Christmas lights, sample German foods, and enjoy tasting wine from the many wineries in the Fredericksburg area. A preview party is held on Friday evening and the tickets allow admittance to events throughout the weekend.

Chapter 7

COOKING WITH
TEXAS WINES

*T*hese recipes feature one or more of the superb wines produced in the Lone Star State. All of them are my family and friends' favorites, and I hope they will also delight you and inspire you to create your own dishes using Texas wines. I've chosen a wide range of recipes including appetizers, salads, chicken, beef, and pasta entrées to let you experience a variety of delectable foods enhanced with the flavors of Texas wines.

None of these dishes are complicated, though some require an investment of considerable time, befitting my outlook on cooking. Cooking for family and friends is indeed an expression of love through the commitment of the cook's time. Over the years, I've come to understand that the most precious thing we can give one another is our time.

A P P E T I Z E R

TEXAS CAVIAR

Preparation time: 2½ hours

This dish has been a huge success at parties over the last few years because it is easy to prepare and tasty to eat while standing around at a party. I can't recall one instance when the plate wasn't completely clean by the end of the evening.

There are numerous versions of this recipe around, but this one has a few twists.

	15-OUNCE CAN BLACK BEANS, RINSED AND DRAINED
3–4	OUNCES CAP*ROCK MUSCAT CANELLI
	4-OUNCE CAN RIPE OLIVES, DRAINED AND CHOPPED
1	MEDIUM ONION, FINELY CHOPPED
3	CLOVES GARLIC, CHOPPED
2	TABLESPOONS OLIVE OIL
3	TABLESPOONS OF LIME JUICE
3	HARD-BOILED EGGS
1	TOMATO, DICED IN SMALL PIECES
1	BOTTLE MILD PICANTE SAUCE
8	OUNCES CREAM CHEESE
	TORTILLA CHIPS OR CRACKERS

In a large bowl, soak the drained black beans in a few ounces of Cap*Rock Muscat Canelli for ½ hour. Drain and mix together with olives, onion, garlic, oil, lime juice, and a touch of black pepper, if you prefer. Cover and refrigerate for 2 hours, stirring occasionally.

Prepare the hard-boiled eggs, cool, and peel. Split only the white of the egg open and separate from the yoke. Set the yokes aside, chop the egg whites, and refrigerate both. Dice the fresh tomatoes and set aside. Remove the cream cheese from the refrigerator half an hour before using.

To serve, spread cream cheese on a plate and spoon bean mixture evenly over it. Place about a cup of diced tomatoes in the

center of the plate forming a small mound. Surround the tomatoes with a ring of picante sauce, then surround the picante sauce
with a ring of chopped egg whites, which should fill the plate
nearly to the edge. Grate or finely chop two of the egg yokes and
sprinkle around the plate. Place the third egg yoke in the center
of the tomatoes. Serve immediately with tortilla chips or crackers.
This appetizer goes well with whatever wine you like.

SALAD

MY SOON-TO-BE-FAMOUS FRESH BEET SALAD

Preparation time: 1½–2 hours

Serves: 6

I wish I could say I dreamed this one up but, in fact, this salad
is an adaptation of one served to us at a vintner dinner in Texas.
I've simplified it and added a splash of wine. For more fun, enjoy
the optional Chardonnay tasting with this salad, which is included after this recipe.

1	BUNCH FRESH BEETS (4 BEETS PER BUNCH)
½	CUP DELANEY CHARDONNAY
½	RED BELL PEPPER
½	YELLOW BELL PEPPER
3	GREEN ONION
	CILANTRO
1	SMALL CAN CORN
1	FRESH CARROT
	OLIVE OIL
	BALSAMIC VINEGAR
	PARMESAN CHEESE

Remove stalks and boil the beets in salted water for 1 hour.
Don't rush the process; the beets need at least 1 hour of boiling
to become tender all the way through. Meanwhile, finely chop
each bell pepper, but don't mix them together. Finely chop the
green onions about halfway up the green portion of the stalk,

and set aside. Tear off a small bunch (about 8–10 leaves) of cilantro, chop finely, and set aside. Drain juice from corn, place in a shallow bowl, pour in the Chardonnay, and set aside in the refrigerator. Pour yourself a glass of Chardonnay and relax while the beets finish cooking.

When the hour is up, remove the beets and let cool for five minutes, then peel. *Be careful; the beet juice will stain everything it touches.* Cut the beets into thin slices (about ⅛-inch thick, if you can), place on a large plate, pour two tablespoons balsamic vinegar over them, and set in the refrigerator to chill—a half hour should be sufficient.

Thirty minutes before dinner, arrange 3 to 4 beet slices on a salad plate. Drain the corn and sprinkle about 10–20 kernels on top of the beets—too much corn will overwhelm this small salad. Sprinkle some red and yellow pepper pieces around the plate, followed by the green onion and top off with just a little of the cilantro for color.

Finally, the carrot! Using a sharp knife, peel the carrot and scrape off shards onto a plate. Sprinkle these carrot shreds on the beets and along the perimeter of the plate. Using the respective bottle caps, pour one capful of olive oil over each salad, followed by two capfuls of balsamic vinegar. Sprinkle a little Parmesan cheese and place in the refrigerator until serving time, but don't let the salads remain in the refrigerator longer than 20 minutes.

Optional Wine Tasting

This beet salad goes especially well with a Chardonnay tasting. Try this if you have enough wineglasses; it always widens guests eyes as they enter the dinning room. Arrange three glasses in front of each place setting before your guests arrive. In advance, chill bottles of Delaney Chardonnay, Becker Chardonnay, and Pheasant Ridge Chardonnay. Before your guests are ready to be seated, cover each bottle for a blind tasting and pour a small amount of wine into their respective glasses. (Try to keep the order consistent from guest to guest; everyone gets confused when you switch the wines around.)

CARNE GUISADA

Preparation time: 2½ hours

Serves: 6

This stewed (*guisada* is Spanish for stewed) beef dish is heavily influenced by the cooks of Mexico. Versions of this dish can be found in Tex-Mex and Mexican restaurants throughout Texas.

1	ROYAL CUT BEEF RUMP ROAST
2	TEASPOONS OLIVE OIL
2	CUPS WATER
2	MEDIUM POTATOES, PEELED AND CUT INTO 1-INCH PIECES
1	LARGE CAN PEELED TOMATOES
1	LARGE ONION, CHOPPED
4	CLOVES GARLIC, MINCED
6–10	BAY LEAVES
½	TEASPOON GROUND CLOVES
½	TEASPOON GROUND ALLSPICE
1	CUP BELL MOUNTAIN CABERNET SAUVIGNON
	5-OUNCE BOTTLE SPANISH OLIVES
½	TEASPOON SALT AND PEPPER

Trim beef, cut into 1-inch cubes, and brown in olive oil. Season to taste with salt and pepper. Pour in water, add potatoes, bring to a boil, cover, and simmer for 1 hour. While the beef is cooking, liquefy the tomatoes and combine with onions, garlic, bay leaves, ground cloves, and allspice and combine in a separate saucepan. Bring to boil and simmer for 30 minutes. Combine this mixture with the beef and the Bell Mountain Cabernet Sauvignon. Cover and simmer for one hour.

Complete this dish by adding in Spanish olives and cook uncovered for another 30 to 60 minutes, or until the broth has reduced and thickened. Serve by spooning over rice or rolling in a tortilla with queso dip.

STEAK TOMAS

Preparation time: 3–4 hours

Serves: 6

The preparation time might seem a bit much to many of you, but trust me, it's worth it. This delicious dish, slow cooked in a broth and wine sauce results in a steak that melts in your mouth. It is best served with rosemary potatoes or cilantro spiced rice and a crispy steamed vegetable. Steak Tomas requires simple presentation, lots of laughter, and plenty of Messina Hof Wine Cellars Reserve Merlot.

4–5	DELMONICO STEAKS
2–3	TABLESPOON OLIVE OIL
1	CLOVE GARLIC, THINLY SLICED
3	OUNCES STE. GENEVIEVE WHITE ZINFANDEL
1½	CANS BEEF BROTH
3	OUNCES MESSINA HOF MERLOT
12	PEARL ONIONS, PEELED AND LEFT WHOLE

Topping

1	MEDIUM ONION, CHOPPED
	OLIVE OIL
1	RED BELL PEPPER, SEEDED AND THINLY SLICED LENGTHWISE
1	YELLOW BELL PEPPER, SEEDED AND THINLY SLICED LENGTHWISE
1	CLOVE GARLIC, SLICED
¼	CUP MARGARINE
1	OUNCE MESSINA HOF MERLOT
8–10	SPANISH OLIVES (WITH PIMENTOS), SLICED
	CILANTRO

Begin by trimming the excess fat off the steaks. Delmonico steaks have enough marbling to provide sufficient flavor. Heat a few tablespoons of olive oil in a frying pan and brown the steaks on each side. Reduce the heat and toss in sliced garlic to brown.

Pour in White Zinfandel, cover, and let simmer until the wine has been reduced by half.

Pour in 1 can of beef broth, cover, and let simmer on low for one hour. Pour in another ½ can of beef broth and Merlot. Cover and let simmer for 90 minutes. If the stock reduces too quickly add in a little broth or White Zinfandel. The remainder of the bottle of Merlot is to be sipped by the cook during the rest of the preparation.

In the final hour, things get busy as you finish the steak and prepare the topping. Place the pearl onions in the pan. If there seems to be too much stock, leave the cover off to allow some reduction; otherwise, cover and simmer for 30 minutes. Use this time to prepare the steak topping.

Steak Topping

In a small saucepan, heat a few teaspoons of olive oil, stir in the chopped onion, bell peppers, and sliced garlic. Cover and simmer on low heat for ten minutes. Add margarine and Merlot and continue to simmer for 20 minutes.

Uncover the steak and add the sliced olives along with three or four cilantro leaves. Increase the heat to bring the stock to a low boil and reduce to thicken it. When the stock has cooked down to one-fourth of the volume, turn the heat to low—you're done! The steak can be served immediately or covered and kept warm until needed.

To serve, place the steak and sauce in a large serving platter and spoon the onion/pepper topping onto the steaks. Messina Hof Merlot will go very nicely with this dish. For the more adventurous, try serving this dish with a tasting of Cabernet Sauvignon from Messina Hof Wine Cellar, Llano Estacado Winery, and Blue Mountain Vineyards.

CHICKEN DISHES

GINGER CHICKEN

Preparation time: 1½ hours

Serves: 4

2–3 POUNDS BONELESS CHICKEN BREASTS
   OLIVE OIL
½ CUP CHICKEN BROTH
1 MEDIUM ONION, FINELY CHOPPED
2 CLOVES GARLIC
1 CUP STE. GENEVIEVE WHITE ZINFANDEL
1 CUP GRAPE CREEK CUVEE BLANC
½ TEASPOON LIME JUICE
2 TABLESPOONS MINCED GINGER
½ STICK MARGARINE
   SALT AND PEPPER, TO TASTE

Slice the chicken breasts lengthwise into ½-thick strips and brown in olive oil. Add chicken broth, onion, garlic, and White Zinfandel. Cover and simmer for 30 minutes. Uncover and add Cuvee Blanc and lime juice. Increase heat and reduce stock to half. Sip on the remaining Cuvee Blanc while watching the stock.

Lower the heat, add the minced ginger along with margarine, and simmer until the remaining stock has thickened and reduced down to just covering the bottom of the pan. If by chance, you've reduced the stock too far, add in a little more White Zinfandel and simmer again. Serve with rice and spoon reduced stock onto chicken. If you cannot find Grape Creek Cuvee Blanc, look for a Texas Chenin Blanc at your local stores.

Stuffed Chicken Breast

Preparation time: 1½ hours
Serves: 4

This easy-to-make dish goes well with either an alfredo-type sauce or a spaghetti sauce (see end of this chapter for my recipe).

2–3	POUNDS BONELESS CHICKEN BREASTS
1–2	CUPS CAP*ROCK CABERNET ROYALE
8	OUNCES SHREDDED MOZZARELLA CHEESE (SEE INSTRUCTIONS)
½	CUP PARMESAN CHEESE
1	EGG
	GARLIC POWDER, TO TASTE
	OLIVE OIL
	MARGARINE
	SALT AND PEPPER, TO TASTE

Trim chicken breasts, flatten, cover with wax paper, and beat with a meat mallet to thin. Place the chicken in a shallow dish. Cover with Cabernet Royale and refrigerate for 30 minutes.

Before using the mozzarella cheese, empty the package onto a chopping surface and finely chop the shredded cheese. I've found this helpful when rolling the mixture into the chicken. Combine the mozzarella and Parmesan cheese with egg and a pinch of garlic powder, mixing together thoroughly.

Remove and drain the chicken breasts, lay flat, and place 1 or 2 tablespoons (use your discretion based on the size of the chicken breast) of the cheese mix on each, carefully rolling the chicken around the cheese. I usually use toothpicks to hold the chicken roll together while baking. Place the chicken in a casserole dish. Brush a thin coat of olive oil on each, sprinkle with a pinch of salt and pepper, cover, and bake for 30 minutes at 350°. Uncover the chicken, place a pad of margarine on top of each chicken roll and bake until browned.

Serve this chicken as it is or with an alfredo or spaghetti sauce poured over it. I recommend either Cap*Rock Chardonnay, Hill Country Cellars Sauvignon Blanc, or Messina Hof's Chenin Blanc to accompany this dish.

FISH DISHES

CRABMEAT-TOPPED SALMON FILLET

Preparation time: salmon: 5–10 minutes; crabmeat topping: 30 minutes

Serves: 6

Salmon is delicious all by itself, but with this rich crabmeat topping, it is incredible. Use fresh salmon and real crabmeat for the best results.

2	POUNDS SALMON FILLETS
	GARLIC POWDER, TO TASTE
	WHITE PEPPER, TO TASTE
2	CUPS FALL CREEK CHARDONNAY
	LEMON AND DILL SAUCE (FROM YOUR LOCAL GROCER)
½	LEMON, CUT INTO WEDGES
1	TABLESPOON LEMON JUICE

Topping:

2	TABLESPOONS BUTTER
4–5	GREEN ONIONS
2	TABLESPOONS FLOUR
½	CUP HALF AND HALF
	SALT AND PEPPER, TO TASTE
¼	TEASPOON TABASCO SAUCE
¼	TEASPON GARLIC POWDER
¼	CUP LLANO ESTACADO SIGNATURE WHITE WINE
1	POUND CRABMEAT
4	OUNCES AMERICAN CHEESE, GRATED
3	OUNCES SWISS CHEESE, GRATED

Place salmon in aluminum foil inside a casserole dish. Add garlic powder, white pepper, and Chardonnay, and coat fillets with a thick layer of Lemon and Dill Sauce. Place two lemon wedges and lemon juice in the pan, cover, and bake for 8–11 minutes at 425° (or use a foil dish and cook on an outside grill). Just before serving, spoon crabmeat topping onto fillets.

Crabmeat Topping

Saute green onions in butter until tender. Add flour, stirring to prevent lumping, then add half and half, salt, pepper, Tabasco sauce, garlic powder, and wine and let simmer for five minutes. Add crabmeat and both cheeses, stirring constantly to prevent lumping or burning. Simmer on low heat for five minutes. Serve immediately on fillets. This dish is complemented by Fall Creek Cascade or Grape Creek Fumé Blanc.

SHRIMP-TO-DIE-FOR

Preparation time: 10–15 minutes

Serves: 6

To be honest, this recipe is my wife's creation, inspired from the time she spent in Louisiana. Although the instructions include steps for baking in an oven, she almost always prepares this on an outside grill. I try to stay away from outdoor grills; everything seems to develop a nice charcoal crust when I cook that way.

½   STICK LOW-FAT MARGARINE
    GARLIC POWDER, TO TASTE
    WHITE PEPPER, TO TASTE
½   CUP LEMON JUICE
2   POUNDS CLEANED AND DEVEINED SHRIMP
½   CUP STE. GENEVIEVE WHITE ZINFANDEL

Melt the margarine in a baking dish and stir in the garlic powder, pepper, and lemon juice and simmer for five minutes. Toss in the shrimp, pour in the White Zinfandel, and bake for 8 minutes on 375°. If you are cooking on the grill, wrap all ingredients in aluminum foil, place onto an aluminum tin, and grill until the shrimps turn pink. Serve as an appetizer or over rice with Spicewood Sauvignon Blanc.

PASTA DISHES

PASTA TUSCANY

Preparation time: 2 hours

Serves: 6

This hearty pasta dish could serve as a meal on its own, but it goes well with meat or chicken entrées. While the ingredients simmer, the house is filled with a wonderfully unique aroma that'll make everyone's stomach growl.

1	MEDIUM ONION, DICED
2	GARLIC CLOVES, MINCED
2	SPRIG FRESH ROSEMARY, FINELY CHOPPED
¼	CUP PARSLEY
1	CELERY STALK, DICED
	CARROTS, DICED
3	TABLESPOONS BUTTER
4	OUNCES GROUND BEEF
4	OUNCES GROUND PORK
2	LINKS SWEET ITALIAN SAUSAGE OR 4 OUNCES GROUND SAUSAGE, IF AVAILABLE
1	CUP BECKER CHARDONNAY
¼	CUP FLOUR
	28-OUNCE CAN WHOLE TOMATOES (PUREE IN ADVANCE)
2	CUPS WATER
1	CHICKEN BULLION CUBE
1	SMALL CAN GREEN PEAS
1	POUND GREEN AND WHITE FETTUCINI
2	TABLESPOONS OLIVE OIL
¼	CUP PARMESAN CHEESE

Combine the onion, garlic, rosemary, parsley, celery, and carrots in a large saucepan with butter and simmer to soften. Mince the beef, pork, and Italian sausage and add to the vegetables and brown slightly. Pour in Chardonnay and allow to simmer for 10 minutes. Sprinkle in flour, stirring to prevent clumping.

Add the tomatoes, water, and crumbled bullion cube. Bring to boil, reduce to a simmer, cover, and cook for 1½ hours. Stir occasionally and add water if necessary. Add the peas 15 minutes before the ingredients have been completely cooked.

Cook and drain the pasta, add in two tablespoons of olive oil, then mix in the other ingredients. Sprinkle the Parmesan cheese on top of the completed dish. This dish goes well with either the Becker Chardonnay or Pheasant Ridge Pinot Noir.

MAKE-BELIEVE GOULASH

Preparation time: 30–40 minutes

Serves: 4

There were few, if any, Hungarian families living in my childhood neighborhood. In an effort to keep four children with voracious appetites fed on a small budget, my mother created what she called "goulash." To us, it sounded exotic and tasted great; to her, it was inexpensive and filling. Now I'm making it for my son.

This is a great dish for the kids or for those evenings when you don't have the energy to prepare a big meal or go out for one. It is easy, fast, and delicious and also tastes just as good after a night in the refrigerator.

1–1½	POUNDS GROUND BEEF
1	SMALL ONION, FINELY CHOPPED
1	CLOVE GARLIC, SLICED
2	CANS TOMATO SOUP
2	SOUP CANS WATER
¼	TEASPOON OREGANO
1	CUP LA BUENA VIDA MERLOT L'ELEGANCE
1	POUND MEDIUM SHELLS OR ELBOW MACARONI
	OLIVE OIL
	SALT AND PEPPER, TO TASTE

Brown the beef with the onion and sliced garlic. Thoroughly mix the tomato soup with water in a bowl, then add to the meat.

Sprinkle in the oregano, pour in the Merlot *l'elegance,* and allow to simmer for 20 minutes. The wonderful aroma coming from this dish is best enjoyed with a glass of Merlot *l'elegance.*

Meanwhile, in a pan of water to which you've added salt and olive oil, boil the pasta *al dente,* drain, and set aside. When the 20 minutes are up, stir in handfuls of the pasta, until there is a good balance between the mixture and the pasta. Add a pinch of salt and pepper, stir, and let simmer for 5 minutes. Serve with the Merlot *l'elegance.*

LA PASTA

Preparation time: 15-20 minutes

Serves: 6

This light dish can be served as a hot side dish or a cold pasta salad.

2	TABLESPOONS MARGARINE
¼	CUP OLIVE OIL
1	POUND ANGEL HAIR PASTA
6	CLOVES GARLIC, MINCED
½	CUP CAP*ROCK DIAMOND ROYALE (SAUVIGNON BLANC)
¼	CUP LEMON JUICE
¼	CUP LIME JUICE
	SALT AND PEPPER, TO TASTE
¼	CUP PARMESAN CHEESE
¼	CUP CHOPPED PARSLEY

Combine the margarine, olive oil, and garlic in a saucepan and cook for 1 minute. Add the Diamond Royale, lemon juice, lime juice, and salt and pepper. Bring to a boil, then pour over the angel hair pasta, toss, sprinkle with Parmesan cheese, and serve immediately.

STUFFED SHELLS

Preparation time: 2 hours

Serves: 6–8

Cheese-stuffed pasta is a weakness of mine. Never mind the pasta shape: shells, manicotti, or lasagna. If it has cheese inside, it's mine. Today this dish can be prepared the traditional way or a heart-healthy way. The two main cheeses used here are now available in a low-fat version.

1	PACKAGE LARGE SHELLS
	OLIVE OIL
	SALT
1	POUND RICOTTA CHEESE
12	OUNCES MOZZARELLA CHEESE
½	CUP PARMESAN CHEESE
1	EGG
1	TABLESPOON OREGANO
1	TEASPOON BASIL
1	TEASPOON GARLIC POWDER
¼	CUP HOMESTEAD MUSCAT CANELLI
	SPAGHETTI SAUCE (SEE FOLLOWING RECIPE)

Boil pasta in water containing olive oil and salt. When shells are done, rinse and set aside. Combine the ricotta, mozzarella, and Parmesan cheese with egg and stir in the oregano, basil, and garlic powder. Slowly pour in the Muscat Canelli, stirring constantly. Chill in the refrigerator for about 20 minutes.

Select only the unbroken pasta for stuffing, setting aside the broken ones for later. Using a spoon (or your fingers like I do), fill each shell to the top with the cheese mixture and place in a casserole containing a thin layer of spaghetti sauce. Top the shells with a small amount of sauce and sprinkle on some Parmesan cheese for presentation. Cover and bake for 30 minutes at 350°.

The broken pasta can be used to hold off famished children who just can't wait for dinner to be ready. Break the pasta into smaller pieces in a small casserole dish. Pour a spoonful or two of spaghetti sauce on top, sprinkle with Parmesan cheese, and heat for a few minutes.

Try serving this dish with Cabernet Sauvignon, or for something different, a Pinot Noir from Pheasant Ridge.

MY SECRET SPAGHETTI SAUCE

Preparation time: 6 hours

Serves: lots of folks for days and days

This spaghetti sauce is a combination of ingredients from at least four different recipes I've enjoyed over the years. The resulting sauce is thick and mildly sweet, despite the addition of Italian sausage. For variety, I sometimes add ¼ pound of ground beef to create a meat sauce. What I like about this sauce is that it never tastes exactly the same each time I make it, but it's always delicious.

3	28-OUNCE CANS WHOLE TOMATOES, PUREED
3	28-OUNCE CANS TOMATO SAUCE
1	12-OUNCE CAN TOMATO PASTE
1	TEASPOON GARLIC POWDER
1	TABLESPOON OREGANO
1	TABLESPOON BASIL
2–3	TABLESPOONS SUGAR
5–6	LINKS SWEET (MILD) ITALIAN SAUSAGE
4–5	LARGE CLOVES GARLIC, CHOPPED
	OLIVE OIL
1	LARGE ONION, CHOPPED
1	YELLOW BELL PEPPER, CHOPPED
1	RED BELL PEPPER, CHOPPED
2	CUPS MESSINA HOF MERLOT
1	CUP MESSINA HOF OR VAL VERDE PORT
	SALT, TO TASTE

Puree the whole tomatoes and combine them in a large pot with the tomato sauce and tomato paste, mixing thoroughly. Stir in garlic powder, oregano, basil, and 2 tablespoons of sugar. Heat until almost boiling, cover, and simmer on low heat for 2 hours. If you are cooking on an electric range, place a spacer between the pot and the stove element to prevent the sauce from burning.

In the meantime, sear the Italian sausage links and 1 clove garlic in olive oil. Simmer on low heat for 15 minutes and set aside, leaving the juices in the pan. Using these juices, add in the remaining garlic cloves, chopped onion, red and yellow bell peppers, and a cup of Merlot. Simmer to slightly soften the vegetables. We're only going to use two cups of Merlot in the sauce. The rest of the bottle is for the cook, so pour yourself a glass and relax for a while.

Next, add the vegetables, Port and Italian sausage to the sauce. Cover and simmer for 2 hours, stirring occasionally. During this period sample the sauce for taste. If desired, add a few pinches of salt. When 2 hours are up, pour in the last cup of Merlot, stir, and sample the sauce. Depending on the taste, you may want to add a bit more oregano and a pinch more sugar. Leave uncovered and simmer for two final hours, stirring often. The sauce can be served immediately, though it tastes even better the next day.

My "Can-I-Have-Some-More-Please" Sausage, Onions, and Peppers

Since it's not necessary to keep all five links of Italian sausage in the previous Spaghetti Sauce recipe, after cooking is complete, you can use a few of them to make a tasty side dish that always disappears when I serve it.

When I visit my Italian friends on New Year's Eve, the family always sits down at midnight to share a plate of sausage, peppers, and onions. The original recipe combined all three in a saucepan with olive oil, garlic, and a pinch of salt—a simple, delicious dish. My version includes some spaghetti sauce for a little extra flavor.

3–4   ITALIAN SAUSAGE LINKS, COOKED IN THE
        SPAGHETTI SAUCE AND SLICED
        LENGTHWISE

2   CLOVES GARLIC, CHOPPED

        OLIVE OIL

1   LARGE ONION, SLICED

1   RED BELL PEPPER, SEEDED AND SLICED
        LENGTHWISE INTO THIN STRIPS

1   YELLOW BELL PEPPER, SEEDED AND SLICED
        LENGTHWISE INTO THIN STRIPS

½   CUP STE. GENEVIEVE WHITE ZINFANDEL

1–2   CUPS SPAGHETTI SAUCE

In a saucepan, brown the sliced sausage links and garlic cloves in olive oil. Reduce heat, stir in the onion, bell peppers, and White Zinfandel, cover, and simmer for 15 minutes. Pour in the spaghetti sauce, cover again, and simmer for 20 minutes on low heat. Serve immediately as a side dish.

Chapter 8

TEXAS WINES IN THE NEW MILLENNIUM

*W*hat's the future for the wine industry in the Lone Star State? Is it all just a fluke? Will Texas wines continue to garner national and international awards, or fizzle with the millennium bug? Will favorable legislation be drafted to allow Texas to compete on an equal footing with other wine producing states? What have we learned about making wine in Texas?

Many in the industry are asking themselves these same questions. Poised at the edge of the twentieth century, vineyard owners and winemakers look to the twenty-first century with a vision based on twenty years of learning, hardships, and breakthroughs. Folks in the industry have learned that what works in California will not necessarily work in Texas. Texas vintners do not, of course, have to start from scratch; many of the techniques and ideas about vineyard production and winemaking are sound. Rather they must learn the proper implementation of these techniques and ideas for Texas conditions, and that has proved to be tricky.

We've also learned that Texas can indeed produce world-class wines on a consistent basis. The vinifera grape (a grape derived from the common European grape) will, in fact, thrive here.

Vineyard managers are slowly learning what grapes will survive where in Texas' numerous microclimates. What works in one area of West Texas may not work fifty or one hundred miles away, even though conditions appear to be basically the same. When we asked Tim Dodd, director of the Texas Wine Marketing Research Institute, what he thought about the future of the industry, he said Texas wines have an enormous potential. He feels that the industry as a whole has to move a notch up, to be competitive within Texas and without. One thing is for certain, Tim stressed, "we need more vineyards." We also need to make the vineyards we have more productive and profitable for the growers in order to encourage increased acreage.

Programs underway such as the campaign to research and conquer Pierce's disease and the Department of Agriculture's Vintage Texas program to market Texas wines lay a solid framework for solving problems and increasing awareness of Texas wine beyond the state.

According to Rick Perry, Commissioner of the Texas Department of Agriculture, "As for the future of the wine industry in our state, I can see nothing to prevent the success of the previous two decades from sustaining well into the next century. Make no mistake that the worldwide market for Texas wines is on the rise. Like the very vineyards necessary for production, the wine industry has taken root in the Lone Star State and will continue to grow."

GLOSSARY

APPELLATION. A United States viticultural district defined as a grape-growing region that has geographic features that make it distinct from other nearby areas.

AROMA. The smells coming from the grape itself rather than the aging process.

BALANCED. When all aspects of a wine come together, no individual feature of the wine stands out.

BIG. A term used to describe a high degree of flavor and body of a wine.

BOUQUET. The scent that wine develops from aging in the bottle.

BOUTIQUE WINERY. A term used to describe a small winery producing quality wines.

BRIX. A density unit based on grams of sucrose per 100 grams of solution. Used for classifying Late Harvest wines.

BUTTERY. A taste that is reminiscent of butter; usually associated with white wines.

CABERNET FRANC. A cousin of Cabernet Sauvignon. The juice of this red grape is usually blended with Cabernet Sauvignon and Merlot. Cabernet Franc lacks the tannin and acidity of its cousin, and produces a softer, lighter colored wine.

CABERNET SAUVIGNON. The most famous red grape in the world, it is planted in every country with enough sun to ripen it. Often referred to as simply "Cab," the grape produces a dark tannic juice that is beautifully enhanced by the vanilla and buttery spices it draws from oak barrels during aging. The young Cab is often harsh, but has an excellent capacity to mature in the bottle.

CALIFORNIA STYLE. From one perspective, the California style is no style, in that, as a young wine region, California is still looking for its own signature style. From another perspective, the California style refers to the modern wine technologies developed in the twentieth century and the experimental nature of the industry.

CHARDONNAY. This green-skinned grape is considered the finest grape variety in the world. In France it is usually blended with Pinot Noir to produce Champagne. Champagne made from 100 percent Chardonnay is referred to as *Blanc de Blanc*. Popular as its own varietal in the United States, this wine benefits more than any other white wine from oak aging. It produces an aroma of figs and apples, an it exhibits a buttery flavor from the oak and malolactic fermentation.

CHENIN BLANC. This green-skinned grape is known for predictable quality. It produces long-lived wines that mature to a marvelous sweetness.

COMPLEX. A wine that imparts many levels of flavor on the palate.

DRY COUNTY. An area in Texas that partially restricts or completely prohibits the sale of alcoholic beverages.

DRY WINE. A dry wine seems to have no sweetness. The yeast in the wine has consumed all the sugar, converting it into alcohol.

ELEGANT. A flavor of wine that is not aggressive to the taste; often used to describe lighter wines.

ENOLOGIST (Oenologist). One who practices the science of viticulture and winemaking.

EUROPEAN STYLE. Best summarized by the word "tradition," it embraces the winemaking techniques that have been used for centuries in Europe. Unlike California winemakers, their European counterparts lack the freedom to experiment with blends of new types of wine. Such actions are prohibited by some European wine control laws.

FAVORITE. Believed to be a cross between the Black Spanish and Herbemont grapes. It is less acidic than the Black Spanish and produces a beautiful dark purple juice. Because of its disease resistance, it holds great promise in south and southeast Texas, with potential for producing a great blush wine.

FINED. A wine that has undergone the fining process.

FINING. The addition of albumen-type substances (i.e., egg whites) to the surface of wine which then descend slowly through the wine taking any solid matter with them.

FRUITY. A term referring literally to the fruit element in a wine. It may be the flavor of strawberry, apple, or figs.

GAMAY. This red-skinned grape is often a source of confusion with the Gamay grape of France's Beaujolais region, which it is not. It is a clone of the Pinot Noir grape and produces light-to medium-body wines.

GERMAN STYLE. Traditional German wines are produced by fermenting the wine until the sugar has been consumed by the yeast. Sterilized grape juice is then added back to a certain level of sweetness.

GEWURZTRAMINER. In German the term *Gewurtz* means spicy, a clue to the character of this wine. It is a white wine that produces a spicy, flowing aroma with a fruity flavor.

HERBEMONT. A grape similar to the Black Spanish (Lenoir) that are both part of the *vitis borquiniani* species. The grapes' aromatics, color, and tannin content are quite different from *vitis vinifera* grapes. The white juice is often used in a dry wine and a semi-sweet amber white.

LATE HARVEST. Refers to the sugar level of the grapes at harvest. Measured in BRIX, Late Harvest wines require a minimum of 24° Brix, while Select Late Harvest wines have a 28° Brix and Special Select Late Harvest require that the grapes be picked at a minimum sugar content of 35° Brix.

LEES. The sediment found at the bottom of a fermentation vessel.

LENOIR. Also known as the Black Spanish Grape, it has been cultivated for centuries in Texas. A thick-skinned red grape that is resistant to disease and the humidity of southern Texas, the grape is used to produce a variety of wine, the most notable of which is the fine Ports made from it.

MALOLACTIC FERMENTATION. A secondary fermentation process that occurs naturally after alcoholic fermentation, when the sugar is converted to alcohol. In this second stage, the harsh malic acid is converted into the softer lactic acid.

MERLOT. A red grape that ripens early producing a minty, pleasant wine. Traditionally used only for blending with Cabernet Sauvignon and Cabernet Franc, Merlot has experienced increased popularity on its own. It offers a lighter, less tannic wine that is drinkable at a young age.

METHODE' CHAMPENOISE. The traditional process used in the Champagne region of France in which secondary fermentation takes place in the bottle. The yeast sediments are then removed from each bottle individually.

MUSCADINE. A native grape of southeastern United States, this hardy disease-resistant grape is a rapid grower. These grapes produce a specialty wine with a distinctive flavor and bouquet.

NOSE. A term used to describe both the aroma and the bouquet of a wine.

OAKY. A slightly sweet vanilla flavor developed by maturing wine in oak barrels.

PETIT SIRAH. Long used as a blending wine this grape produces a dark, high-tannin wine with an aroma of spices.

PHYLLOXERA. A louse that attacks vine roots, sucking the life out of the plant.

PINOT NOIR. This red-skinned grape has long been a component of French Champagne. It is often referred to as the "headache grape" because it is difficult to grow and work with. Less tannic than Cabernet Sauvignon, this dark-colored wine often costs more than other varietals because of the extra expense of growing the grape.

RIESLING. A white wine. Normally produced in a sweet style, it is sometimes found as a dry wine.

RUBY CABERNET. A clone of the Cabernet Sauvignon grape developed in California. Ruby Cab has a better color, is less acidic, yet has a strong Cabernet-like character. It is mainly used for blending with Cabernet Sauvignon and Cabernet Franc.

SAUVIGNON BLANC. Traditionally used as a blending wine, it has seen recent popularity when made dry and unblended. Sauvignon Blanc is sometimes referred to as Fumé Blanc, referring to the use of a short oak aging to remove the grapes' sometimes grassy flavor.

SEMILLION. Resistant to vineyard diseases and producing a good yield, this white grape has struggled to be popular with winemakers in America. Thin-skinned and susceptible to rot, this grape can produce a honeyed, apple-and-cream flavored dry wine.

SPICY. This term describes a range of flavors from exotic fruit to peppery or clovy.

SURLIE. French for "on-the-lees." The term describes a wine that is left with the lees in the same container during part of the fermentation.

SYRAH. Producing a smoky, rich flavor, this wine historians believe originated in what is now Iran, near the town of Shiraz. Australians today call this wine Shiraz. Normally used as a blending wine. When used unblended, it requires careful control and aging on oak.

TABLE WINE. Usually the lowest tier of a winery's products, these low-priced wines are made for immediate consumption. These wines are often labeled with generic names such as Chablis, or Rose.

TANNIN. This bitter, mouth-puckering part of red wine is derived from extended contact with the skins and stems of the grapes. It is crucial to a wine's ability to age in the bottle.

TRELLIS. The system of wood or metal stakes and wires used to support the grapevines.

VARIETAL. A type of wine named after the primary grape in a bottle. For example, a bottle of Cabernet Sauvignon must contain 75 percent by volume of wine made from the Cabernet Sauvignon grape.

VINIFERA. A species of grape also known as Old World or European. Varieties belonging to this species produce more than 90 percent of the world's grapes.

VINTNER. A person who makes or sells wine.

WINE STYLE. Refers to the characteristics of the grapes and the winemaking techniques. There are so many variables in making wine that winemakers can create many styles from the same grape variety.

WOODY. A flavor brought about from the aging of wine in wood barrels.

ZINFANDEL. This grape produces fine, robust red wines. Most Zinfandel finds its way into "White" Zinfandel, which is actually a pink wine. True Zinfandel wines range from rich, intense flavors to light, fruity wines. Made almost exclusively in the United States, this chewy, mouth-filling wine is finding increased popularity.

INDEX

ABOUT THE AUTHORS

Thomas and Regina Ciesla are active travelers and avid wine buffs. As 20-year residents of Houston, Texas, they were in a position to watch the Lone Star State wine industry develop from a few pioneering winemakers to one of the fastest growing wine producing regions in the country.

This husband and wife team spent 4 years traveling the state to study every aspect of its wine business. They met the owners and staff, attended seminars, and they tasted the wines. In 1995, they created the Wines of Texas web site at www.neosoft.com/~scholars/texas.htm. This site was voted one of the top 100 Texas web sites in 1996 and 1997 by *Texas Monthly*® magazine.

An architect and computer consultant by trade, Thomas was fascinated with the science and art of winemaking. Regina, a software consultant, shared his enthusiasm. A burgeoning wine industry in their own backyard was a terrific discovery; and, while the couple was almost reluctant to share their find, they decided it was too good a secret to keep.

Join the authors for a journey through Lone Star State wineries, and discover a delightful taste of Texas life.